A Primer on Business Analytics: Perspectives from the Financial Services Industry

A Primer on Business Analytics: Perspectives from the Financial Services Industry

Yudhvir Seetharam

INFORMATION AGE PUBLISHING, INC.
Charlotte, NC • www.infoagepub.com

Library of Congress Cataloging-In-Publication Data

The CIP data for this book can be found on the Library of Congress website (loc.gov).

Paperback: 978-1-64802-818-2
Hardcover: 978-1-64802-819-9
E-Book: 978-1-64802-820-5

Printed in the United States of America

CONTENTS

DEDICATION

To Shehlangoma Frans Manganyi.
A comrade, a friend, a colleague.
Thank you for your service, Lieutenant.
Rest In Peace

ACKNOWLEDGEMENTS

The mocker seeks wisdom and finds none,
but knowledge comes easily to the discerning.

—Proverbs 14:6 (NIV)

As with any arduous task, it is best to accomplish it a step at a time. When I started off my career as a data scientist, that phrase did not exist. Now, over the years of observing and gathering insights, I hope that my practical explanations can help others discern what to do, when to do it and how to do it. The world of numbers is fascinating, but in isolation, is actually not valuable. It only unlocks potential when combined with action—creating actionable insights.

This book is dedicated to those past, present, and future data scientists. Those who have a passion to pursue truth in the midst of volatility, uncertainty, complexity, and ambiguity.

To those who supported me through this journey, I thank you. You know who you are and the role you have played. Ranging from my most critical critic to the most encouraging and supportive ones. To my team at FNB, thank you for your support and invaluable experiences which have made this a reality. To my colleagues at the University of the Witwatersrand, thank you for the comments and feedback in writing this book.

PART 1

UNDERSTANDING BUSINESS ANALYTICS

Business analytics, in the context of the 4th Industrial Revolution (4IR), is the "new normal" for businesses that operate in this digital age. It is imperative for business owners to understand the power of data and analytics to survive and thrive in times where uncertainty, driven by the 2019 Coronavirus pandemic, can cause unexpected interruptions to the daily running of businesses. The first part of this book explores the history behind analytics, which may surprise many readers as the buzzword will be revealed to be a term used for the past few decades. We then unpack analytics in the context of banking, introducing many topics that are relevant for those in the financial services sector. We then explore some human capital thoughts on how to set up and manage an analytics team, given the global skills shortage of this role.

CHAPTER 1

INTRODUCTION

We have moved to an age where the art (or science) of analyzing and interpreting numbers is no longer reserved for the "nerdy" of society. Over the last decade, there has been exponential interest and effort dedicated to data science to solve real world problems. While there is a more technical definition of the term "data science," it is easier to think of it as the application of scientific principles (from mathematics, statistics, and computer science) to data to produce actionable insights. What are actionable insights? They are facts (or information) that enable the person who asked the question, to answer the question. Insights without action result in "fun facts"—facts that are interesting to know, but which do not shape our decisions. Action without insights is akin to doing something with no purpose.

LEARNING OBJECTIVES

After reading this chapter you should be able to:

- Have a broad understanding that analytics is not new;
- Understand the corresponding areas linked to analytics; and
- Appreciate the potential value in using analytics to solve problems

A Primer on Business Analytics: Perspectives from the Financial Services Industry,
pages 3–8.

HISTORY OF ANALYTICS

The notion of collecting and analyzing data has been around longer than the popularity of the function itself. Consider Figure 1.1 from Delen and Ram (2018). It shows that both hardware and software developments into what is today known as analytics started as early as 1970. As technology developed rapidly over the corresponding decades, so too did the emergence of techniques to analyze data. Figure 1.1 however does not consider the relevant development of mathematics and statistics—as these were crucial inputs into developing the hardware and software that followed. For example, in its simplest form, a neural network (discussed in Part 2) is simply a collection of algorithms based on mathematical and statistical principles. Therefore, the development of analytics cannot be seen in isolation from the development of its foundational aspects. Analytics only recently became known as data science—the art (and science) of analyzing data to produce insights that solve real-world applications.

Figure 1.1 shows that the evolution of analytics cannot be separated from the linked concepts of Information Technology, Business Intelligence and as mentioned above, advancements in empirical techniques. These can sometimes become overwhelming for those wishing to enter the field. It is helpful here to recall the definition of producing actionable insights. It is sufficient, but not necessary, to use advanced empirical techniques in the production of such insights that can help solve problems. In turn, these advanced empirical techniques are reliant on computational power. Therefore, development in one area (enhancing techniques) is restricted to the theoretical realm until such techniques can be implemented with the alongside development of computational capabilities. In the 1970s, the concept of Artificial Intelligence (AI) was not new (as seen below and again in Part 2). However, the AI of the 1970s would pale in comparison to the AI of today. That does not mean that the "older" AI was insufficient in solving the problem posed to it, but rather it "did the best it could" with the available resources at the time. These Decision Support Systems were created to assist users to answer relatively simple questions and to enhance efficiencies in tasks that were manual (at the extreme example, calculating on an abacus compared to calculator and then compared to Microsoft Excel). Once these simple tasks could be optimized, attention turned to the desire to see and identify trends. The rise of Business Intelligence around the 1990s propelled the need for many executives to drive their

FIGURE 1.1. The Evolution of Analytics (Adapted From Delen & Ram, 2018)

companies forward based on the data (trends) available to them. Again, with further developments in computational capabilities, the competition amongst companies then needed a further disruptive factor—that of prediction. It was no longer good enough to see trends, but to rather forecast or predict said trends (and over time, corresponding actions) for executives. This gave rise to the "era of analytics" and concurrently, the phrase "big data" became more popular.

DEVELOPING BUSINESS ANALYTICS

When data science is applied in a business context, it can also be referred to as "Business Analytics." As such, someone who works in the analytics field can have a variety of names—some refer to them as data scientists, others as quants, and others with a variety of either lesser known or newly formed roles (such as data engineering or data analysts). Indeed, when looking at the data spectrum, it is natural for a specialization of roles that are suited to perform different tasks. Faced with a tough global economic climate, financial institutions, and businesses in general need to leverage off the power of analytics. Some developments of the past 5 years include:

1. Data science can now be studied at university.
   Naturally with the hype comes an increase in awareness of data and how collecting and analyzing it can offer benefits to a business. Given the specialist skills required for these roles, universities are now introducing (or have already) analytics degrees—effectively preparing the future generation to function in the analytics world once they begin their working career. This trend is more prominent in developed economies than emerging ones. For example, South African universities have only started to offer data science curricula over the last 3 years.
2. Data science is now visible.
   Data is only useful if it produces some positive outcome, where positivity is measured against the ability to answer the question posed. Simply storing it becomes meaningless until, at the very least, a report showing trends is produced. The simple act of visually seeing data will increase, as more analysts utilize simple (or even commercialized) software to display data to their stakeholders. A surprising role reversal will occur—instead of a stakeholder asking for data, they will be provided with insights that can then be actioned. We introduce another role here—that of a Business Intelligence (BI) Analyst. Many battles have been fought between quants and BI stalwarts over defining the difference between the two disciplines. Some think of BI as being a simple visualization role, others see it as providing insights (derived from data using empirical principles) to enable better decision making. If defined as the latter, the line between the roles of a quant and BI become blurry.
3. Businesses are now legally obliged to manage it.
   To mitigate the impact of potential financial crises, regulators are enforcing stricter management of data, especially in financial institutions. For example, a recent addition to the Basel accords—a form of banking regulation—is that

banks need to have accurate and reproducible credit reports. This means that a bank needs to prove to a regulator that what's in its reports can be backed up with data. Similarly, to avoid the misuse of data, many countries are adopting data protection and privacy standards—in the UK it is referred to GDPR, in South Africa, as the POPI Act. This act protects the consumer's personal information from misuse by any business.

4. We are now part of the data-driven age.

   We are living in an age where we become more connected to electronic platforms—from social media to kitchen appliances. By essentially creating your own "home" web, you can easily order groceries online (or your fridge can do it for you), automatically record your favorite episode on TV and even watch over the house while you're on holiday. The glue that holds these webs together is known as the "internet of things." Arguably, this data reveals much about your preferences, which can (properly) be used to find suitable products that would make your life easier.

5. Data can be profitable

   From a business perspective, being able to understand the customer is key to both survival and profitability. Businesses are investing more capital into analytics and data, to derive customer insights—how they can understand the preferences of their customers. While financial institutions are on this band wagon, we still have a long journey ahead of us to truly understanding our customers to offer tailor made solutions to them.

Despite positive case studies and the increasing uptake of analytical capabilities by large businesses, some Small and Medium Enterprises (SMEs) are still skeptical. Indeed, the analysis of data subsequently sparked the buzzword known as "Big Data." Big Data refers to large amounts of data that is often complicated, unstructured and has the potential to add insights to a particular problem. For example, if a business were to use your social media profile to advertise certain products to you, that is one means of using big data to produce insights to a business (when should they display an advert to you), ultimately requiring them to take action (to sell you a product). Businesses initially (and still do) have some common misconceptions about data.

1. Data (big data) is a fad.

   Some small businesses are still of the opinion that big data is just a fad that will soon fade away. A small clarification is needed here -while the term "big data" may not be as popular now as it was a few years ago, the idea of digitalizing, of using data in a meaningful and insightful way is definitely here to stay. While holding onto tradition is valuable in some instances, business owners need to also observe the landscape around them. Just as new competitors appear on the scene, so too can competitors use data to optimize or disrupt the market. The returns of a data-driven strategy are also not necessarily immediate—those expectations need to be managed so that they pay off in the long term (if investing in infrastructure) but can be realized in the short term if "quick" questions can be answered via data. When applied appropriately and in context with the nature of the business it can become a major competitive advantage. Businesses should also consider the way the data is collected, processed, and analyzed to produce strategic insights from it.

2. The data journey requires substantial investment.

   Advancements in technology have enabled any business regardless of size to gain access to state-of-the-art Big Data analytics tools. This has been instrumental in removing barriers to the use of Big Data which was previously limited to large organizations. An SME can easily get off-the-shelf tools that help optimize their business and provide some ideas on disrupting their market. Investment here is either technology based (which will have decreasing costs over time), or people-based (finding a data scientist is easier said than done!)

3. Only large corporates need big data.

   As a small player you still need insights on your customers as well as market dynamics to take your business to the next level. These simple, often overlooked measures are often the key to optimizing your business in the short term. SMEs mistakenly assume that Big Data is only effective when massive data sets, dating back several years are analyzed. The emphasis should not be on the amount of data you have as a business, but rather insights that can be derived from it.

4. It's not relevant for my sector.

   Although some industries have had greater successes with Big Data, such as the health care and financial services industries, any business that has access to data can leverage this tool. Moreover, it's never too late for a small business to start collecting data for insights. For example, opening a social media page where customers can interact and provide feedback on the business' products and services.

5. Our data is not complex enough.

   The biggest misconception that exists is that valuable insights can only be derived from complex data sets that can only be analyzed by qualified data scientists. While, this notion may be true for some industries, data does not necessarily need to be complex to be analyzed. A handful of likes on Facebook about a certain product range over a period, can provide a lot of insight to a small business.

Big Data and Analytics is certainly not a fad. Small businesses that are still skeptical should consider doing research or consulting an expert to determine how it can potentially benefit their businesses. Further, businesses need to understand the difference between simply progressing down the data journey versus being progressive in running their business—you want to spend the most amount of effort where it counts, as opposed to just following the herd.

CASE STUDY

The following case study is based on the recent events of 2020 and the onset of COVID-19.

The Coronavirus disease (COVID-19) is an infectious disease caused by the newly discovered coronavirus in 2019, that has rapidly spread across many countries. It spreads through water droplets in the air and is highly contagious. As of 2021, many countries are implementing vaccination programs to help curb the spread of the disease. Many countries had a "lockdown" where movement of the human population was severely restricted to minimize contact with each other, thereby increasing the risk of transmission from one person to another. It has caused a crippling effect on the economies (present and future) of many nations.

> In many countries, it became paramount to measure (historically) and predict the number of positive infections to enable better management of the pandemic. Given the question of "when should I move my country into lockdown," leaders of nations needed to see a report that showed not just historical figures but also predictions. We can divide this question into 1) gathering data of sufficient quality; 2) interpreting and presenting said data and 3) modelling the future infection rate. In the early stages of the new year, there had to be logistical processes in place to ensure that medical laboratories could not just identify correctly (known as a true-positive as opposed to a false-positive) but also timeously. This data then needed to be submitted to a central agency in the government for collation across the various labs conducting these tests. The central agency would then collate this data and visualize it for insights to be provided to government. Government officials would have the ability to observe trends daily, with any further views (such as per geographic area of the country) at their fingertips. If the data was not classified or had all available demographic information, it is easy to see the repercussions of such decisions being taken on the back of "bad data." Last, the infection rates needed to be forecasted to allow decisions to be made. However, at the early stages of the pandemic, there was simply not enough data to make reliable forecasts (in the realm of statistics, this is referred to as an adequate sample). Only once more data became available, could the accuracy of such predictions also increase. Thus, many governments had to make tough calls on national (or more localized) lockdowns based only on a handful of data that potentially could not be of high quality.

In your opinion, do you think the decision-maker should wait until more data is available or make decisions based on what data is available (regardless of its quality)?

QUESTIONS

1. What do you think is the difference, if any, between a quantitative analyst and a data scientist?
2. How has analytics developed over the past year, because of COVID-19?
3. Think of 5 different industries or sectors and how they use analytics to enable actionable insights.

CHAPTER 2

THE APPLICATION OF BUSINESS ANALYTICS

LEARNING OBJECTIVES

After reading this chapter you should be able to:

- Gain insights to the different analytical domains within banking
- Link the output of analytics roles to the success of a business

(BUSINESS) ANALYTICS IN BANKING

The application of analytical methods to the banking sector is far from new. Banks serve two primary functions—as a deposit taker (allowing the public to save/ invest funds) and a lender (allowing the public to take out credit). These two functions come with accompanying financial flows. If a customer deposits money with the bank, the bank's liabilities will increase, and it will pay a particular interest rate to that customer. If a customer borrows money from the bank, the bank's assets will increase, and the customer will pay a particular interest rate to the bank. In maintaining profitability, the bank should ensure that the rates paid are less than the rates received. Further, banks are usually supported by a central bank (which acts as regulator, amongst other functions). Therefore, the interconnected

A Primer on Business Analytics: Perspectives from the Financial Services Industry,
pages 9–26.
Copyright © 2022 by Information Age Publishing

nature of banks is such that money will flow between them (only), thus creating a "money multiplier" effect, coined in economics.

Banks therefore must ensure that their rates are both competitive and profitable. As such, two functions emerge where analytics are required—pricing and credit origination. The pricing function is largely based on optimization algorithms, where the price given by a bank on an interest rate (or even on the monthly fee), is a function of a particular customer's behavioral patterns, as well as the internal costs faced by the bank. The credit origination portion predicts which customers qualify for credit, based on internal as well as external data. Customers who apply for credit with the same bank that they have a current account with already have "provided" the bank with their behavioral (income and expense) patterns. This data, along with external data sourced from a credit bureau (which aggregates any credit taken out per customer across multiple financial service providers), are used as input into a scoring model. The scoring model predicts the credit quality of the customer, and the bank then decides on the appetite it has for lending to customers across the quality spectrum.

Along with credit origination is the sister-function of capital and provisioning. At the heart of the matter, the credit origination model aims to predict quality, but circumstances may change and, as a result, customers may miss a payment (or multiple payments) on their loan with the bank. As such, banks need to have reserves in place for when defaults occur. Second, banks need to ensure that they have adequate capital funds if there is a "run" on the bank—when those with deposits decide to withdraw unexpectedly. The analytics needed in this function are quite closely aligned to that of credit origination but come with the added complexity of abiding by regulations (such as the Basel accords). Relatively untapped functions are risk management (the prediction of fraud and anti-money laundering practices); and Financial Resource Management (an "advisory" function to internal departments of the bank units of how to maintain revenue and reduce costs). The former is more "traditional" in the sense of banks needing to safeguard their customers against illegal activities conducted by (cyber) criminals. The latter is necessary to provide a macro-perspective of how the bank is managing its balance sheet and income statement in order to remain stable, especially during uncertain times (such as the onset and succeeding years of the COVID-19 pandemic).

The next most popular analytical function relates broadly to "customer analytics"—the ability to sell the right product at the right time to the right customer via the right channel. Customer analytics is truly where innovation in analytical techniques, as well as creative approaches and ideas are needed for banks to thrive in a competitive landscape. A typical customer analytics function comprises of:

1. Acquisition analytics—how to acquire more customers to the bank (such that they have a current account).
2. Sales analytics—post acquisition, what are the necessary products/services needed based on the customer's lifecycle.

3.   Financial optimization—as the customer's lifecycle progresses, there are natural pushes from the bank to enable cheaper means of transacting. Customers are therefore incentivized (via reward programs) to transact via less expensive channels—for example, transacting via the bank's online banking platform instead of going into a branch.

4.   Research analytics—the quantification of a bank's market share, share of wallet, and other "qualitative" data sources, such as customer experience. This area is traditionally housed in a marketing environment yet is substantially driven by analytics.

The above customer analytics functions are not unique to banking. Indeed, running a business successfully can be summarized as the actions that result in increased profitability (through higher revenues and/or lower costs). As such, analytics is not a function limited to banks, but to any business.

DATA-DRIVEN PROFITABILITY = DATA-DRIVEN CUSTOMER EXPERIENCE

For any entrepreneur, running a business often requires multi-tasking across multiple functions -such as marketing, sales, operations, risk, and financing. Each of these areas requires tactics and strategy to optimize their contribution and "fitting together" to ensure that businesses survive and thrive. Further, each of these areas has data at their core as a shared trait. In this digital age, managing customer relationships inevitably equates to having a good understanding and use of the data. Therefore, the successful running of a business requires clear strategy, focused direction, and efficient execution. As is often the case, either the details (the translation of strategy into tactics) are unclear or the execution is poor. Businesses must consider the value of data, unlocked by analytics that can be added to its operations to both survive and thrive.

While the above is true for nearly any business, those in the banking industry are required to understand and treat their customer fairly, as this relationship is deeply rooted in trust—banks are custodians of our wealth, meaning that loyalty often is the deciding factor in a successful banking relationship. Typically, a bank (business) would need to define the following four key areas.

1.   What is the hook? What attracts customers to your bank?
      Often, the hook relies on a customer's perception of your bank, which then needs to be met once they start a relationship with you. In trying to identify the hook, analytical use-cases from the realm of marketing, acquisition and research play a role. These use-cases can help answer questions such as:
      a.   What is the size of the target population?
      b.   What percentage of this population hold a current account with me?

    c.   What percentage of this population would I like to bank?

    d.   What draws customers to bank with me?

    e.   How do I identify prospective customers who I wish to bank?

    f.   How do I acquire these targets?

Once your prospective customers have been "hooked," it is necessary to ensure that they have and use appropriate products that are offered by your bank. Banks face one of two challenges for newly acquired customers—how do they increase their sales, and how do they increase their revenue. Selling accounts is great for achieving targets, but unless the account is activated and used regularly, revenue generation is non-existent. Analytics use-cases on financial behavior as well as sales assist here, as they drive customers to have the right revenue-generating behavior—a win-win scenario for both the customer and bank.

2.   Cross-sell/up-sell.

For those banks who offer life-stage specific products, it is not just a case of getting customers to buy once-off, but to instead buy repeatedly. More so, as the customer progresses through their life-stage journey, the bank should be able to identify and offer products that are relevant for that stage. For example, for a newly married couple, it might be necessary to offer them property financing, as it might be observed that newlyweds purchase property. This form of cross-selling is key, as it enhances the customer's satisfaction with their bank, as well as enhancing lifetime value.

3.   Optimization.

Throughout their banking journey, customers can sometimes stray off the "chosen" path. Banks are well on the digitalization journey, thus requiring customers to also digitize with them. The revenue obtained from the previous stages enables organizations to invest in technology that enhances and sometimes simplifies the bank's offering to its customers. This form of innovation—optimization—can and should lead to a more favorable cost-to-income ratio.

Optimization is a missing ingredient that many banks miss, as they focus instead on disrupting the offering made to customers in the hope that their business will grow. For banks to thrive in the digital age, it is necessary to optimize, thereby gaining cost-efficiencies, while at the same time looking for opportunities to disrupt (innovate) in the product market offering. Throughout this "fly-wheel," sales, marketing, and product development, all underpinned by analytics, need to work closely together to ensure a holistic customer experience. Banks must ensure that what attracts customers to them (via marketing), is sold to them (via sales) and lives up to their expectations (via product development). Perhaps the easier department to revolutionize with data and analytics, is marketing.

THE (R)EVOLUTION OF DIRECT MARKETING

Having re-established the basics of running a business (bank), attention must now be given to how banks can attract and retain customers. Direct marketing—the individual communication of a bank with each of its current and potential customers—has also evolved over time, both in form and in function. Initially, direct marketing could be linked bank to travelling salesmen—where a business' sales force would walk the streets stopping at each house to offer their wares. This strategy caused much anxiety for recipients, as either they were cajoled into products they did not want, or they already had the product that was being sold to them. Fast-forward to the mobile age, where emails and text messages are being used to spam customers—with much the same result (albeit at a cheaper cost than a travelling salesman!) This spray-and-pray approach, where businesses would "target" as many potential leads as possible hoping for a conversion, is both a money-draining mechanism and a terrible customer experience.

With the use of logic, data and some intuition, direct marketing has evolved to segment target groups, personalize messages, customize offerings, and individualize the approach. These forms of "hyper-segmentation," where a bank gathers enough data to offer the right product to the right customer at the right time via the right channel, pays enormous dividends when executed correctly. Underpinning direct marketing is the analysis of data. Banks can build models that can predict the likelihood of a customer taking up a product based on a variety of behavioral factors. These, when coupled with a model that chooses the customer's preferred means and time of communication, has an extremely high rate of success. Again, this speaks to the link between what's best for the customer is best for the bank. We thus start to discuss how analytics can help a bank manage the value gained from customers.

CUSTOMER VALUE MANAGEMENT (CVM)

CVM, broadly defined, speaks to how a bank maintains its relationship with customers, with the goal of increasing and/or maintaining the value of that relationship. It requires the bank to not only to offer the right product to the right customer at the right time via the right channel, but to also ensure that the customer is using the products they have. Value is therefore only extracted from this relationship when the customer has been sold an appropriate product that increases the strength (retention) of their relationship with the bank. A useful metric for measuring CVM, at a strategic level, is known as Customer Lifetime Value (CLV). CLV is calculated as the present value of future net income for customer i, scaled by the likelihood that customer i will stay with the bank.

As you can see, CLV requires both a financial metric (future profits) as well as a customer-specific metric (a retention rate).

Calculating CLV

To calculate the retention rate, you need to calculate the probability of a customer *leaving* the bank (the attrition rate). Attrition models are quite commonplace in banking today; and are built according to a "standard" recipe. Before we use the retention rate, we will briefly discuss some concepts of attrition in banking.

Attrition in a banking context refers to the loss of customers from the "register" of the bank. If a bank started the year with 100 customers, and by the end of the year 30 customers no longer have a bank account with the same bank, the attrition rate is 30%. Calculating this figure is relatively straightforward as demonstrated with the above example as it relies on historical data. However, a historical rate is just that—it does not inform the CEO of how many customers are in danger of leaving in the future. As such, there is a need to predict an attrition rate (a probability) per customer, to then allow the relevant sales teams to identify critical customers who require intervention to remain with the bank. In doing such a prediction, there are nuances that must be considered, which then lead the data scientist to accurately predict this rate for each customer.

First, the data scientist must define the target variable. Defining attrition is perhaps the most difficult as if this is ill-defined, the entire process of retention is at risk of failing. When defining attrition, one must be careful to consider:

1. What you can observe versus what you intend to measure.
    In the context of retail banking, if an account closes, it can be due to the customer switching to a competitor, or for regulatory reasons (such as suspected fraud) or quite simply the customer passing away. In the business banking context, businesses close their bank account to either switch to a competitor, or due to the business failing. These reasons may not be directly visible in the data, making attrition difficult to predict. The data scientist should consider the various reasons for account closure, to then determine which of those reasons can be feasibly modelled.
2. It's all about the timing
    Second, the data scientist must consider the time frame of the prediction. Are you predicting whether a customer will close their account in the next second, or the next day/month/year? This time frame must be chosen to be appropriate from both a modelling perspective (to ensure high predictability) but also from a business perspective (no bank can act within the next second to save a customer!)

Once the target variable is defined, the traditional methodology of building a model can be followed. Once the model is built and tested statistically, the final phase involves execution of the output. A sales force would be able to action the list of high probability attrition customers to then provide feedback on whether the model achieves its objectives. When deciding on which customers to retain, it is important to prioritize this dataset for the sales force. This can be achieved by ranking the high probability customers by each customer's individual profit to the bank. This allows the sales force to focus on high "net worth" customers, defined as their predicted probability scaled by their current relationship value to the bank. Notice here that the attrition model, which resulted in a prediction per customer, was ranked according to a financial metric. This allowed the bank to focus on which customers currently are valuable, which need to be retained. We can slightly change this thinking when returning to CLV. CLV will therefore allow the bank to see the impact of actions taken per customer. It is, ironically, a metric that shows the impact of the past.

The retention rate that we need in the CLV model is simply the remaining probability from the predicted attrition rate (as probabilities must add to unity). By building a model that predicts the probability of attrition for each customer, we have indirectly also calculated the probability of retention for each customer.

The first term of the CLV is the present value of future profits. Each customer is worth some value to the bank. On the strict assumption that the bank can accurately determine this profitability, we would need to forecast it to determine future value. Forecasting profit can be achieved through time-series methods, via hazard functions, via artificial intelligence and so forth. In forecasting, it is important to have reasonable assumptions of how far into the future one must forecast, and which growth rate(s) are applicable based on that horizon. For example, it is reasonable to assume that a retail-banking customer will stay with the bank until they pass away. You can then use actuarial life projections to determine this time horizon per customer. Based on both current and future economic conditions, as well as the stage of the individual's life, you can make reasonable assumptions of their future wealth (and update these as life conditions change). Once you have these future profit values, simply discount them to the present using an appropriate discount rate (which can be the Return on Equity value for your company, or the rate used by the Finance Department in their project budgeting process, or even inflation!).

The final CLV calculation is the result of those the multiplication of those two terms of retention and present value. Obtaining a CLV per customer is useful when you want to see the impact of actions on a customer. The retention factor can be influenced by sales of products, by customer experience and service; whereas the profitability factor is influenced by the transactions made by the customer, the payment of monthly fees and how they use the bank's products. If, for example, a bank wants customers to use digital payment solutions, it is easy to see that this will impact current revenue. However, if this results in a greater retention rate, one should see an increase in CLV. You can therefore use CLV to focus on key activities that must be achieved with the customer from a CVM perspective.

Propensity Models

Similar to attrition models, product propensity models supply a probability that a particular customer will take up a particular product. They are built in much the same way as described previously. However, when the output of the model needs to be executed, it is important to understand the preferences of communication with each customer when these campaigns are executed. A customer may prefer to be sent an email or message as opposed to a phone call. These customer preferences are important in determining the overall success of the campaign. A campaign is successful only if the (1) product, (2) sales conversation and (3) appropriate set of customers are successful. It is unfortunate that many view campaign failures as the "fault of the data," when in fact the product may not be appealing, or the salesperson simply was not convincing enough! Therefore, when judging the efficacy of product propensity models, one must be careful to measure this success against the right data. For example, if you are measuring success against the product being taken up, the product may take 3 months to be fulfilled! This does not mean that the model incorrectly identified appropriate customers, but rather that the fulfilment process of this complex product is what caused the take up to be "low" after 1 month of measurement.

Banks may also build channel propensity models that can rank the appropriate means of communication. This largely applies if a customer has opted in to multiple means of contact, and it would be beneficial for the bank to pick not only the most cost-effective channel, but also the channel that will most likely influence the take up of the product.

It is easy to see the benefit of building the above models for each product and across channels available. One additional layer of complexity must be introduced when there are multiple product propensity models that all want to communicate with the same customer. We must now move from a product-centric way of thinking to what is holistically beneficial to the customer.

MOVING FROM PRODUCT-CENTRICITY
TO CUSTOMER-CENTRICITY

This analytically driven customer centricity should be at the heart of any successful bank. If one were to group customer interactions simply, one can then decide on the most appropriate strategy to communicate with customers.

Consider Figure 2.1. A customer of a bank will either initiate a conversation with the bank (for either a sales or post-sales (operational) reason); or vice-versa. In other words, either the customer first talks to the bank (customer initiated), or the bank first talks to the customer (bank initiated). When interactions are customer initiated, the bank must ensure that through all of its customer facing channels (such as ATMs, branches, telephony and digital banking), the bank is able to profile the customer interacting (have descriptive information on the customer), is able to rank the customer's value (so that actions or suggestions to offer products

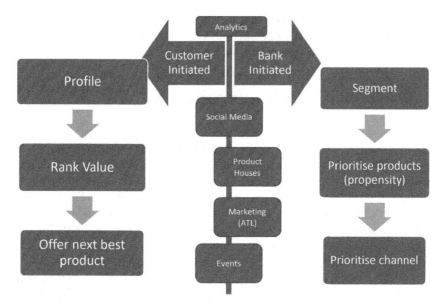

FIGURE 2.1.   Customer Value Management Analytics. (Source: The Author)

and change behavior are prioritized) and must be able to offer the next best product to a customer (if a customer takes up a product, the next most closely associated product should follow. For example, offering a credit card and sign up for a
rewards program, where credit card transactions are rewarded). This last action
is done especially well by online retail giants, where usually before the end of a
purchase, there is an option to see similar products or what else customers bought
along with the primary product being purchased). Profiling and value ranking are
important as while each customer is important to the bank, some are more valuable than others—a rather contentious but true statement. This does mean that
service levels should change based on importance, but rather that the bank should
know which customer they are dealing with to offer the most expedient service
and advice.

In the second category, that of bank-initiated interactions, data is used in a pro-
active manner. Customers need to be segmented to provide insights into potential
value propositions (grouping of products and services for a single fee), along with
propensity models being developed to help prioritize products and channels. This
stream is normally where direct marketing efforts can clearly be seen to (not) pay
off, based on the level of analytics developed.

Regardless of the initiation of the interaction, banks are foundationally run using data. These interactions can then branch out into social media as a means of
interaction, into events where the public (inclusive of customers) can interact with
the brand and over above-the-line media (such as radio, TV, or billboards). Even

when a bank has the right process in place, it must ensure that what is promised to a customer can be delivered—customers are often quite happy to pay for products and services that they perceive as valuable.

CUSTOMER CENTRICITY

The above framework is useful when a business has a range of products to be sold to customers. From a banking perspective, there are typically five main categories of products—transactional, lending, investing, insuring and value-adding/ rewards. These five "pillars" often holistically solve for a customer need by producing a solution that solves for the problem faced by the customer. For example, a customer who wishes to buy property would require lending solutions, possibly insurance solutions and reward or value-adding solutions (such as registering the property on your behalf). Value-adds, as they are called, are meant to reduce the effort taken by a customer in typically administratively burdensome tasks.

While you may have propensity models per product, as well as for a preferred channel of communication, you face the situation of which products to prioritize over others. The simple way of prioritizing is to simply rank according to executive decision. This however does not cater for what the data show, which ultimately will lead to a sub-optimal solution for a customer. There are some solutions that data can provide.

1. To standardize the output of each product propensity model
    A product propensity model provides a distribution of probabilities between 0 and 1. When this distribution is compared to another, there is a possibility that the distributions are not statistically similar. For example, a propensity distribution for a credit card model may have values clustered between 0.7 and 0.8; whereas a propensity distribution for an investment account model may have values between 0.6 and 0.7. If we consider the same customer who appears in both distributions, we may incorrectly conclude that the customer would first take up a credit card and then take up an investment account. We first need to standardize the output from both models and then rank them.
2. To use clustering techniques in determining an appropriate solution
    Some analytical solutions are available that allow the user to observe patterns amongst variables. For example, Market Basket Analysis or, more fundamentally, clustering, can be used to determine which combination of products are typically held by customers. This input can be used by executives to determine an ideal value proposition (a basket of products and services that are appropriate for a particular type of customer). These clustering techniques offer advice on what the current market basket comprises of your existing customer base. There is still a need to

crosscheck this result against what should be in the basket—do not fall into the trap of correlation and causation! If the existing basket of products speaks to 3 of the 5 pillars, it does not imply that the ideal basket only consists of 3 pillars.

3. To rank according to appropriate metrics

We have already covered CLV as a metric. Others can include the revenue per product (where higher revenue products are prioritized), or efficiency metrics (products that are fulfilled quicker are prioritized). These metrics are used as both a reward for those departments that perform well and an incentive to those under-performing departments to improve their operational processes. We expand on this last point below.

EXPECTATION VS DELIVERY

If a bank can market effectively, sales should increase. However, marketing is one component of ensuring that the sale is "banked." The other element speaks to the ability of the bank's systems to handle the increased volumes in an efficient manner. Further, one must also take note of what a customer expects and what the bank can realistically deliver. In South Africa, it was uncommon for banks to offer credit on a near real-time basis until a few years ago. This data communication between banks and credit bureaus allowed them to assess a customer's credit score in a matter of seconds before making them an offer. With optimizing systems also comes the disadvantage of increased customer expectations—if we are in the digital age, customers may expect account-opening processes to be as quick as possible, which may not be achievable by the bank. The first question to ask is if the bank is simplifying the right processes—has each step of the account opening process been scrutinized and questioned for efficiencies. Second, once this has been prioritized and executed, the bank needs to determine if it is meeting customer expectations. Sadly, statistics in this area are quite rare. Figure 2.2 is a snapshot of a study done by a South African research company, which investigated the account opening process of various products in the business banking space in South Africa. As can be seen, the level at which expectations are met vary across the major SA banks, with only one performing "better than or at" expected levels. This either means that customers have low expectations of Bank 4, or that Bank 4 is doing well to meet and exceed its customer's expectations. These expectations are usually established by the branding of the bank itself to attract and retain customers; banks usually resort to catch phrases or slogans that speak to their audience in an empathetic way. This double-edged sword is where some banks fall, along with believing that innovation purely means doing something that disrupts the industry, as opposed to also viewing innovation as a form of optimization.

Expectation

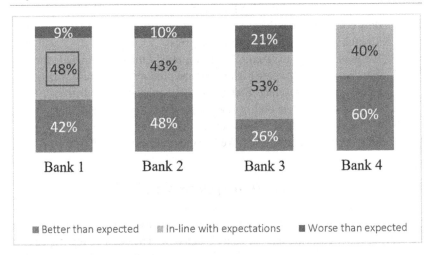

FIGURE 2.2. An Example of a Turn-Around-Time Survey (Source: The Author)

UNPACKING INNOVATION

According to Bower and Christensen (1995),

> Generally, disruptive innovations were *technologically straightforward*, consisting of *off-the-shelf components* put together in a product architecture that was often *simpler* than prior approaches. They offered *less of what customers* in established markets *wanted* and so could rarely be initially employed there. They offered a *different package* of attributes valued only in emerging markets remote from, and unimportant to, the mainstream.

Innovation, a necessary characteristic for businesses to both survive and thrive, has sometimes been misunderstood to cater only for disruptive practices—based on questions such as, "what new product or service should my bank release to the market to increase my market share?" However, going back to the seminal work on the matter, Bower and Christensen (1995) explain that disruptive innovation is normally what mainstream customers do not necessarily find important. In other words, it is initially secondary to the main product offering.

Banks thus forget that innovation has both a disruptive component as well as an optimization component—often required to reduce costs and become as lean as possible, prior to freeing up cash flow for research and development purposes. Disruptive innovations are therefore required in industries to prompt existing market players to question their efficiency. These innovations are normally cheaper (such as offering a no-frills bank account), are more accessible to the public (such as via digital channels) and have some structural cost-advantage (such as not having massive infrastructure or branch costs, in the case of banking). These innovations are identified by entrepreneurs who truly understand the industry, often supported by insights off the back of (big) data.

The customer experience journey is an ever-changing one—one that requires an intimate knowledge of what a customer expects and what they experience. Closing this gap is no longer the ambit of marketing or product or even operational divisions, but also with the assistance and support of analytics. Executives responsible for customer experience need the right data about what's happening in their business to then decide which initiatives to undertake that simultaneously reduce cost and increase customer experience.

CUSTOMER EXPERIENCE

Customer Experience can and should be the "bridge" between current profitability and lifetime value of customers. Consider a simple example of using Uber, the transport service app. When ordering "an Uber," you as a prospective customer want the effort to be minimal. Once you get into the car, you want the journey to be satisfying. These two factors, effort, and satisfaction work together to create a great customer experience and often increase the loyalty you have towards that service (in the sense that you will use it again). Good customer experience is synonymous with customer loyalty. Often, we are primed to maximize our satisfaction in the present, but this needs to be tempered with a forward-looking view to ensure that those customers come back yet again to recreate that great experience.

Many businesses have focused on the "Single View of the Customer" (SVC) towards the late 2010s. While the idea sounds attractive—that of creating a holistic, 360-degree view that shows you everything you need, the first problem many encounters is a lack of definition. What exactly is a holistic view of a customer at a bank? At the very least, it should consist of data from various departments within the bank—customer, account, transactional. When you consider external data, the options are much wider, as it speaks to what *currently* is beneficial to enhance the banking relationship versus what *could* enhance that relationship. The never-ending amount of data being produced in the world makes this a never-ending quest to find relevance. This perhaps personifies the balance between experimenting (testing and thinking which data will be beneficial) and prospecting (knowing data will be beneficial and trying to acquire it).

At the very least, an SVC should comprise of all available internal data that provides a holistic view of a customer. Chipping away at this stone is achieved by the maturity of your customer analytics function—understanding customers to be able to increase lifetime value and product holding. Personas or hyper-segmentation have become popular concepts but remain in their infancy given the lack of fully defined SVCs. Creating personas for your customers enables you to understand where they are in their customer journey, and consequently retain them as they move from point to point. Hyper-segmentation provides granular level insights that assist in the "conversation" you have with customers, as it allows you to deeply understand their needs, wants and preferences during interaction. The ideal world of banking is no longer limited to loans and investments. It has expanded to become a world where the experience of the customer is at the heart of every interaction at every successful bank.

Measuring and managing customer experience requires an understanding of where a customer is on their journey with the organization. Simplistically, at the point of sale, the customer is acquired to the organization. It is important to understand what they did (and even did not!) take up. Most banks offer a holistic product basket (a solution or a value proposition) to attract non-banked clients to them. For example, if you are young professional, a bank will offer an appropriate Young Professional value proposition that offers a set of products and services that are considered attractive to that target market. If, at the point of acquisition, that entire value proposition is not taken up, this either means that the target market does not match what is being offered, or the entire value proposition is not being offered by your sales staff. In ensuring that you have value propositions for your customers it is important to not over- or under- sell appropriate solutions to them.

Once a customer is acquired, there is usually a fulfilment and entrenchment process that kicks off. This ensures that customers have access to what they signed up for, have activated what they signed up for, and are actively using what they signed up for. This is the second major phase of a simplistic customer journey. If a customer does not pass this phase, it points towards either technological inefficiencies in giving them the solution or activating the solution; or that the solution offered and accepted was not really needed at that time (as it would have been activated immediately if it were).

The third phase of the journey speaks to growing, maturing, and retaining your customer. As a young professional becomes older, they potentially enter a different phase of life (such as getting married). The solutions required for a married individual are not the same as a young professional. Thus, starts the journey again, with the difference that you "upgraded" the existing value proposition to another one, for the ultimate benefit of the customer.

As the customer progresses through their journey, you as an organization can measure their experience at points of it. The feedback obtained can then be used to increase efficiencies or to create/offer alternative solutions. For example, if you find that customers expect an account to be opened within 10 minutes, but it takes you 30 minutes, the corresponding efficiency identified can then be assessed and implemented in the corresponding department. By mapping the customer journey, you can then choose interactions to measure, obtaining feedback on whether you are meeting expectations or not. This ultimately leads to an increase in lifetime value, as you are both offering relevant products and simultaneously decreasing the chances of your customer leaving for a competitor (as they feel valued).

Let's now define Customer Experience (CX). At its heart, a great customer experience leads to increased loyalty—if you felt good while doing/after doing something, then you would want to do it again! We can simplistically view CX as two components—how much effort did you take in doing a particular task and how much satisfaction you received after the task was done. In the context of banking, this can be achieved through direct or specific feedback from the customer (where you identify particular customers and ask particular questions) along with generic or anonymized feedback where your target group is not restricted to those who bank with you. The direct feedback is naturally more controlled as the organization can identify key interaction points as described previously to measure and proactively manage. However, this restricts your feedback to those who already bank with you. For you to identify why someone does not bank with you, it follows that you need to cast a wider net!

BEHAVIORAL BUSINESS BANKING

In recent years, there has been a significant move by many banks towards a more integrated and holistic view of banking customers than just consumers of banking products. This so-called 'behavioral banking' trend sees financial institutions offering products and services that are specifically geared towards enabling the lifestyles and aspirations that customers have, while also offering a variety of incentives and rewards for behaviors by customers that have the potential to improve their health and lower the risk they present to the financial institution.

The behavioral banking model relies extensively on being able to collect and analyze data on each individual customer in order to build up a psychographic profile that provides a clear view of their behaviors and habits, and allows the financial institution to then target products, services and incentives to support positive lifestyle and money management changes.

Unsurprisingly, given the mutual benefits this banking model unlocks, it has proven very successful for the banks that have implemented it, and is becoming increasingly popular among retail banking customers. But retail is only one, relatively small, component of financial services; and most banks have extensive business banking clients that not only make a significant contribution to their bottom line but have far more complex banking and finance needs than most individual banking consumers.

All of which begs the question: "can the retail behavioral banking model be adapted for business banking clients and, if so, would the benefits created for those businesses make behavioral business banking a compelling proposition for them?"

The answer, I believe, is an unequivocal yes. But unlocking the full value of a behavioral business banking model for entrepreneurs and business owners requires that banks change their view of what a business is. The truth is that a business is not just buildings and annual performance figures. If it was such an inanimate object, there would be no point trying to integrate behaviors into the business banking services offered to it. Rather, it's vital to recognize that every business began because of the vision, dream, or passion of a person. And even the most successful, or large, business is still ultimately the product of such human vision and endeavor. When a bank can shift its understanding of a business in this way, the possibilities of adding value to the business, and the bank, through a behavioral banking approach become very clear.

And it's not just the business banking clients that stand to benefit from behavioral banking. From a bank's perspective, the imperative to move into the realm of such value-adding behavioral business banking is also becoming increasingly urgent. As new banks enter the South African market, and fintech partnerships rapidly evolve and mature, the banking environment is becoming more competitive than ever. What's more, business banking offerings are now highly commoditized, with little to differentiate one bank's product from that of another. Against this backdrop, asserting yourself as a leading business bank requires the reinvention of the way you service your clients—and behavioral business banking undoubtedly presents an opportunity for this level of differentiation.

Of course, the effectiveness of such a behavioral banking service rests primarily on the bank's ability to make an emotional connection with the owners or directors of the business in order to tailor the business banking products and services to meet their distinctive needs, as well as optimizing the financial services needs of the business entity. The aspirations and desires of these business owners are what ultimately give the business its character.

More importantly, the financial habits and behaviors of business owners often shape the money management approach and behaviors of the business. So, for example, FNB's value proposition for its business clients is to be their most trusted financial partner. Delivering on this promise is not possible if all they do is provide basic business transactional banking and off-the-shelf lending products based on the numbers at the bottom of a financial statement. We need to look beyond the business operations and gain an understanding of the people and behaviors that give it its character—and then maximize the business value we add by positively impacting on those entrepreneurial and financial behaviors.

All of which means that the essence of behavioral business banking is not trying to change the business; its fully understanding, and partnering with, the people that make the business what it is. And when a bank makes this fundamental shift in the way it views its business banking offering, the value it can add is unlimited. Not just by offering incentives and rewards, but also by working with the business owners and their employees to identify behaviors and actions that could be detrimental to the company's financial 'wellbeing,' and help to replace those behaviors with good, rational, alternatives. Achieving this level of behavioral banking effectiveness is a certain way for any bank to elevate its position from a transactional service or product provider to a true business-building partner.

CASE STUDY

Read and watch the material on the links below.

https://www.ibm.com/blogs/business-analytics/banking-analytics/
https://www.spssanalyticspartner.com/industry-solutions/financial-services/

Tough Lessons Learnt From Nedbank's Pepper

August 2018

Introducing Nedbank's fully programmable humanoid robot, Pepper, to the South African market has been a steep learning curve for the Old Mutual-owned bank.

This is according to Fabio Mione, head of NIC and strategic execution at Nedbank, speaking at the Meeting of Minds: ITWeb Artificial Intelligence 2018 conference, held today in Johannesburg.

Mione discussed what the bank has learnt since launching SA's first humanoid robot in March.

"We've had some real tough lessons since Pepper's introduction a few months ago, but we are working towards resolving the challenges we have encountered," explained Mione.

Pepper, developed by Japanese corporation SoftBank, uses artificial intelligence (AI), to provide clients with basic information around Nedbank's products and services, such as helping them understand how to lend, invest, and save money.

Based at the bank's digital branch, NZone at the Sandton Gautrain station in Johannesburg, Pepper communicates verbally and can evolve its skills and give feedback accordingly. It also responds to touch, environmental and tablet input, and is interactive, progressive, and autonomous.

"One of the lessons that came out of our observations is that Pepper can be easily distracted when communicating with clients. Because she has many sensors on her, it can be a challenge to get her to focus only on the person engaging her. She sometimes gets distracted, when there is too much movement around her, resulting in her stopping the conversation halfway to focus on another client.

"Furthermore, Pepper has limited engagement time, which means she requires a break after two-and-a-half hours due to sensory overload. She also uses phonetic programming to speak, so we have to adjust the words that are programmed in the dictionary, by spelling them differently for her to get the pronunciation right, especially when speaking vernacular languages."

Despite these challenges, the bank has seen great value in having Pepper in the branch, especially where self-service is concerned, Mione pointed out. The bank is focusing on improving clients' experience with Pepper, through upgrading the customer engagement aspect.

"One of the big headers we've seen from Pepper is her helping people understanding how to download and activate the Nedbank app on both Android and iOS stores. She also provides information on our cash-accepting ATMs and this has probably been Nedbank's greatest value from Pepper so far."

In future, Pepper will be able to provide other types of financial-related information, by using artificial intelligence to search an Internet-based database and provide information such as interest rates in real-time, he continued.

When not engaging with clients, Pepper is usually in the hands of the IT team, in a developing state, resulting in limited time spent with clients. Due to this, Mione noted that Nedbank is considering adding two more similar humanoid robots that will alternate while the other is being programmed.

"One of the things that have surprised us has been how intimidated and nervous some people feel about initially engaging with Pepper. So we have to coach them a bit, but once they start talking to her, we find people coming back up to six times to have different conversations with her, so we are definitely looking to add more Peppers in future," he concluded.

https://www.itweb.co.za/content/Kjlyrvwdj8W7k6am

QUESTIONS

1. Using local banks as an example, rank each bank on your perception of their use of analytics.
2. How does this rank compare to their brand value?
3. If you were asked to start the analytics function within a bank, what are the key areas of analytics that you would first explore?
4. You are tasked to measure Customer Experience for your bank. Discuss some of the key principles and provide examples of metrics you would use to achieve a simple, yet effective measure of Customer Experience.

CHAPTER 3

THE HUMAN RESOURCE BEHIND BUSINESS ANALYTICS

The businesses that will be able to count themselves amongst the most successful in the coming years will be those that have succeeded in fully harnessing the power of data. But while you'd be hard pressed to find many businesses that are not currently building or acquiring systems and technical resources aimed at unlocking the value of data, the same priority does not appear to have been given to embedding data-driven organizational cultures.

LEARNING OBJECTIVES

After reading this chapter you should be able to:

- Understand the impact of culture on the success of a business.
- Understand the need to have specific employee value propositions for data scientists.
- Gather insights on the impact of COVID-19 to data science careers.

A DATA-DRIVEN CULTURE

This failure to focus on culture in parallel with technology not only reveals a lack of understanding of the symbiotic nature of the relationship between the two, but

A Primer on Business Analytics: Perspectives from the Financial Services Industry,
pages 27–36.
Copyright © 2022 by Information Age Publishing
27

also presents a real risk that the massive investments being made into data might not deliver the returns that companies are hoping for.

The problem lies in the fact that while analytics and processing are relatively exact sciences, a data-driven culture is significantly more difficult to define. While company owners, managers and executives may not be able to tell you exactly how data science works, they can tell you what they want to get out of it. The same is not true of their understanding of a data-driven culture, and so the creation of such a culture is either assigned a lower strategic priority, or simply handed off to the organization's Chief Technology Officer, Chief Data Officer or HR executive.

This approach is unlikely to unlock the full value of being data driven. To do that, every person in the organization must recognize the importance of being fully data-driven as a competitive differentiator and embrace the need to build a data-driven culture within that organization.

This is by no means a small ask. Apart from the significant challenges—both technical and human—that a business is bound to face *en route* to becoming truly data-driven, it's likely that every person in a company has little to no idea of what the concept of 'culture' actually means in a company, let alone what a data-driven culture looks or feels like.

And that's why the process of transforming a culture to be data driven must begin with the end in mind. That, of course, begs the question.

What Is a Data-Driven Culture?

Unfortunately, there is no simple answer as every business is different and will have different culture parameters. However, it is relatively safe to say that, irrespective of how businesses look or work, their data-driven cultures will have a few things in common.

For one, a data-driven culture will be built on the broad recognition of data as a vital, strategically essential business asset; one that allows the business to make well-considered decisions based on facts and figures rather than on intuition or past experience. Having a data-driven culture will also mean that the business fully recognizes and embraces the ability of data and its application to empower all employees to perform their functions much more effectively. And lastly, a business will know that it has completed its transformation to a data-driven culture when it is able to identify and align its technical and business challenges and leverage data to solve both together.

When you consider these factors as characteristics of a data-driven culture, it becomes obvious that being data-driven is not solely a technical strategy. So, while it is important to recruit skilled and talented data scientists and technology professionals to give physical effect to the data-driven vision, trying to become data-driven in isolation from the business and all its other employees is almost certainly a recipe for failure. Which brings me to the second obvious question that will, or at least should, be asked by every business that wants to be able to unlock the full potential of data as a transformative, business-building asset.

How Do We Do It?

This, too, is a simple question without a simple answer. Most of the global organizations that are considered to have succeeded in becoming data driven still admit to being in the learning phase when it comes to embedding a data-driven culture. Here are some typical steps that businesses, and especially financial services organizations, need to take to move closer towards achieving a data-driven culture.

The first of these is to start by transforming thinking. You need to get the entire leadership body to commit to supporting and promoting a data-driven culture. Even if very few of them understand what that means, a good first step is to simply get board and executive management agreement to being willing to embrace a culture of openness and collaboration.

Then, with that leadership support, start to communicate with the entire organization to create an understanding of the meaning and value of being data driven, both for the company and its employees and customers. Ultimately, any shift in culture is only possible when culture is mainstreamed. It cannot be the domain or responsibility of HR. So, an organized and strategic education campaign is essential to explain the benefits that embracing a data-driven culture will provide.

The next step is to commit to democratizing data. When employees have access to data, its impact becomes obvious. Break down silos and protectionism. Ensure that data, and its analyses, are readily available, understandable, and transparent across the organization.

Obviously, it's dangerous to just give everyone in the organization unfettered access to all its data since they probably don't have the skills or tools to make use of that data. And that's where the real culture shift happens or must happen. Businesses need to focus on building collaborative, multi-functional teams. While tech experts may understand the technology and systems, data is first and foremost a business asset. A data-driven culture must be driven by the business. And since it's unlikely that you're going to find too many employees with a balanced combination of business and data skills, you need to build your data-driven culture on collaborative teams in which every team member is willing to acknowledge what he or she doesn't know and work closely with teammates that do. This approach should also inform all future recruitment decisions. In a data-driven culture, you don't recruit just to fill a vacancy, but to make teams stronger.

Finally, be patient. Changing a company's culture takes time, effort, and commitment. Even when the leadership sets the example, the shift only happens through organic growth and evolution. Realize that there are legacies that must be changed. The technology legacy systems are the easy part because you can throw money at those. But human legacies around how things have always been done in the past are much more difficult to shift. But it must be done, because it is impossible to change to a data-driven culture if all your people are not willing to recognize and embrace data as a key success facilitator.

The Benefits of a Data Driven Culture

While the need to build these types of data-driven cultures is becoming increasingly obvious, the unexpected, and valuable, side effect of achieving such a culture is that it has the potential to massively enhance employee morale and productivity. That's not just because data-based decisions are infinitely more effective than those based on hunches. It's also because employees grow as people when the work, they do have meaning.

Data can quantify the impact that each employee has on customers and the business. And when staff see the tangible value of the contributions they are making, they become far more connected to the company values and their own professional goals, and the result is incremental improvements in personal performance and, of course, bottom-line results.

Hiring a Data Scientist

As more businesses realize the benefits of using Big Data to produce strategic insights and key decision making, there is a growing need to invest in the appropriate skills. Given the massive amounts of data that businesses produce, coupled with the rare technical skills needed to derive valuable insights from it, the role of Data Scientists who are able to leverage this raw information into a competitive edge has never been more important.

Here are a few tips for businesses that are looking to hire Data Scientists to assist them with their Big Data efforts:

1. A clear objective—Businesses that appoint Data Scientists prematurely will not only waste money and resources, but both the employee and organization's time. It is important for management to be clear about its objectives (what do they want out of the data) and adequately assess the needs (when do we need it; and why do we need it) of the organization before an appointment can be made.

2. The right skill sets—While most data scientists major in technical field such as mathematics, statistics, or computer science, a one size fits all approach will not suffice when appointing the best individual for the business. The candidate will be required to possess an additional set of skills depending on the industry or role they will be filling. Typically, Data Scientist need to have a mixture of technical and "business"-related skills—they need to "number crunch" and explain what they have done (including the value of it) to the layman. For example, a data scientist in the financial services industry would require more some basic knowledge of how a business operates, to truly understand the business prob-

lems, they are hired to solve. Alternatively, for an individual specializing in agriculture where data would predominantly be utilized to increase operational efficiency of farming and predict weather patterns—a more risk-return analysis, process improvement and Agri-based skill set would be relevant. This is one of the reasons why there is currently a shortage of Data Scientists globally -do these elusive people even exist, and if they do, where can businesses find them? According to IBM the demand for data scientists will soar 28% by 2020, which is already off an incredibly high growth rate. The company further stated that by 2020, the number of jobs for all US data professionals will increase by 364 000 openings to 2 720 000. Although South Africa is still lagging, we can expert similar trends in the future. It becomes clear that we will have the demand, but is there a supply of data scientists to choose from?

3. Hiring at the right level—A business that is starting out in its Big Data journey is better suited appointing a less experienced scientist who would collaborate with data experts within the organization while refining their skills. While this may seem counterintuitive, the balancing act remains to find someone who is willing to learn, and skilled enough to contribute to your business. Furthermore, given the challenges of finding the right talent, it would also be viable for organizations to invest in candidates at university level and groom them as future data scientists for their organizations.

4. Upskilling internally—Businesses who find it challenging to attract data scientists externally should consider training existing employees who already have the advantage of understanding the business, provided they have some aptitude for quantitative-type work. Again, this is somewhat of a risky tactic, but given the skills shortage we face, it might be the most viable option for smaller businesses.

Once the ideal individual has been appointed, the most important consideration for businesses should be retention, given the high demand for this rare skillset in the industry. For the data scientist to produce actionable insights and enjoy problem solving, they must be invested in the organization for the long-term.

THE OUTLOOK AND CHALLENGES FOR DATA SCIENCE AS A CAREER IN A POST-PANDEMIC WORLD

It's universally agreed that one of the most significant changes that have been brought about by Covid-19 is the significant shift in the way people will live and work in the years to come. Given that technology and digitization will be central to this shifting dynamic, the role of data scientists in enabling and informing business strategy has never been bigger or more important.

Against this backdrop, one would be forgiven for assuming that data scientists now pretty much have built-in job security as businesses transition to a future characterized by robotics, artificial intelligence and the ability to effectively leverage data to gain a full understanding of the desires, expectations and preferences of their customers.

However, while it's true that jobs in the data science realm will probably be more readily available and more secure than many other positions over the next few years, this doesn't necessarily mean that a data science qualification automatically guarantees you a comfortable and secure career. The simple truth is that no jobs are 100% secure in the current economic environment. As second waves of the virus begin to take hold across the world, many industries continue to face severe challenges, and companies of all shapes and sizes will be required to take whatever steps they can to avoid bankruptcy. For many, these steps may well include layoffs and retrenchments, and data scientists, analysts and engineers are by no means immune from the impact of such business decisions.

That said, data science was a good career choice long before the ravages of Covid-19, and it will almost certainly continue to be after the virus has been dealt with or brought under control. However, as with any career decision, it is essential for a prospective data scientist to consider more than just a conducive environment when making the choice to pursue a data-focused career path, whether that is a first career or a change in existing profession.

One of the most important considerations is that, as companies are being forced to take a far more cost-sensitive approach to the way they operate, they will increasingly be looking to get more bang for every buck they spend. Talent is no exception, and many organizations will be focused on bringing only the best skills into the business or drawing from their existing talent pool rather than looking outside it. What's more, where more value can be achieved by outsourcing data analytics, there's a strong possibility that businesses will do that in order to lower the cost to company often associated with having to employ large teams of in-house data experts.

Obviously, this means that there may well be significant opportunities for aspiring data scientists to join fintech's and other data services providers, but competition for these positions is still likely to be fierce. The other absolutely vital consideration for anyone thinking about entering the world of data science is that the current working environment makes it very difficult to get an accurate view of the culture of a prospective employer, or whether you fit well within that culture. Of course, this is true for anyone going into any position that is currently operating remotely, but the nature of data analytics, and the very close working relationships on which successful data science teams must be built, makes culture fit a vital consideration when accepting a data-related position.

Unfortunately, while digital connectivity has made it relatively easy for data scientists to complete tasks collaboratively, it's not possible to experience the true organizational culture of a place or team when you're not able to immerse yourself in the physical workplace. Which means that, unless you really do your homework around company culture before accepting a job, you could be in for a shock when the time comes for everyone to fold up their tracksuit pants and go back to work.

In the end, there's no doubt that the changes brought about by Covid-19 mean that undertaking, or switching to, a career in a data science field is likely to provide the individual with numerous opportunities in the years to come. However, that doesn't mean that one should simply throw caution to the wind when making potentially life-changing career choices.

Future growth in demand for data scientists is inextricably linked to economic and industry forward momentum and the ability of businesses to reach a position of sustainable growth once again. For most, the data scientists they already have will certainly be instrumental in getting them to that position. But it's likely that only once most arrive there, they will start to look seriously and actively to build those data science teams by means of external recruitment. While it's not possible to say exactly when that will be for every business, it's almost certain that the day will come—at which point the supply of qualified, well-rounded, business-minded data scientists is unlikely to be able to keep up with global demand.

BUILDING AN ANALYTICS TEAM

Perhaps the most controversial topic for any data science field of inquiry is on who should be a data scientist! Should it be someone with technical skills only? With business acumen mixed in. With no experience in the role? I try to keep things simple by stating that a data scientist must have a mixture of technical skills and business acumen. This unfortunately does not correlate to the size of the business that requires this skill, its age, or even its stage in its lifecycle. It is primarily driven by the objectives (vision) of that business. If the leadership of a business is not sold on the idea of being a data-driven organization, then they should look for someone who is more business oriented to start this function. While that requires significant delivery of analytical projects in a short space of time, the "basics" achieved can often hint to leadership of a greater need for this function. Thus, the organization of your data science team is based on the appetite of the business to be data driven.

For data science teams who are past the "startup" stage, the next phase is to rapidly expand. This requires many supporting roles over and above the data scientist. These roles can broadly be classified under the role of data engineers. First, let's define a data scientist, before we define a data engineer.

A data scientist is an individual who can utilize methods from mathematics, statistics and/or computer science to produce insights for the organization. Based on this definition, the first requirement is for the data scientist to have some background knowledge on empirical methods. This can be achieved through a variety of courses and not necessarily degrees. Remember, you need someone who can learn and adapt to new techniques as they are created; and that does not necessarily mean that you need someone with a Ph.D.! I also use the word *courses* to emphasize that the individual needs to be proficient in empirical methods, not a master at it (go back to that point on learning!)

Second, a data scientist must be able to communicate. Communication can take the form of being verbal, written, or visual. Again, you do not need to be proficient in all three, but the choice of which one is needed is dependent on the goals of the organization. An organization that has just started the data journey will be amazed by simple visualizations (story telling), whereas an organization established in data will expect more.

Third, the data scientist must have the ability to be curious or passionate about their field. Often, data scientists want to move jobs without really knowing whether they will be a fit for that field or not. As an example, credit risk is primarily driven by regulation. That means that room for creativity is not as wide compared to a data science role in sales.

Given those three characteristics, data scientists can be assigned to "back office," "middle office" or "front office" roles, based on their fit and performance. Naturally, front office roles deal much more with business stakeholders, who do not regularly know how to "speak data." It thus requires someone with more people management skills than a back-office role. Middle office would be the "production" environment, where they would receive request from front office

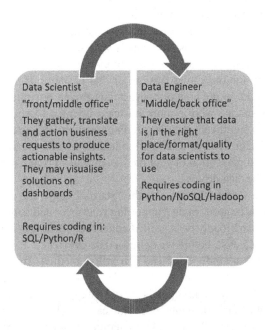

FIGURE 3.1.   An overview of a Data Scientist and Data Engineer Role (Source: The Author)

to automate or productionalize projects. Back-office roles are much closer to the IT side of data, having a deep understanding of systems, technology, and their interplay with data.

As such, data engineers are typically back office or middle office roles. They are the bridge between the source system or data warehouse and the data scientist. In contrast, data scientist roles can be front office or middle office oriented.

Figure 3.1 is a diagram that summarizes the skillsets of a data scientist and a data engineer. The two roles work closely with each other to deliver on viable and sustainable requests from the business. Often, data across an organization is not readily available or of high quality. The data engineer is primarily responsible for ensuring that data is ready to use by the data scientist. They ensure that systems that generate data feed into a data reservoir, is ultimately of high quality and is governed according to data quality and information management principles. They do not typically deal with requests or require an understanding of business. In contrast, data scientists are much closer to business stakeholders, often receiving requests, translating them into data requirements and executing on such via some model. The output of the model can be visualized, enabling the data scientist to tell a story from the data.

CASE STUDY

First National Bank (FNB) South Africa identified the need of hiring and retaining talented data scientists, in line with global human capital trends in 2017. The bank conducted a review on its data scientists, concluding that they need to offer 5 elements to them, to retain talent. These 5 elements were: Career Development, Community, Compensation, Contribution and Communication. These "5C's" were packaged into an employee value proposition that offered new and existing data scientists the opportunity to grow their career in an organization that embraced data and its value within its culture. The Career Development component created promotion criteria, outlining the specifics needed for a data scientist to progress from junior to senior, to management. These criteria were built with the data scientist in mind, often nudging individuals to grow not just in technical skills, but to become more importantly ingrained in the running of the bank. The criteria focused on 5 key competencies—technical skills, business understanding, strategic awareness, leadership skills and stakeholder relationships. A data scientist needed to demonstrate mastery in accordance with the promotion they were applying for. Over 3 years of implementing the criteria, the retention rate increased significantly (from 60% to 70%), along with the sunk cost of replacement being minimized (a typical replacement would cost nearly R380 000 per individual, inclusive of labor costs and higher salaries of the incoming individual).

QUESTIONS

1. What are the advantages and disadvantages of a technical specialist being promoted to a manager?
2. What are the ideal characteristics of a Chief Data and Analytics Officer?
3. Is it even feasible to retain data scientists given their high salaries? Should this function not be outsourced?

PART 2

TECHNIQUES USED BY THE DATA SCIENTIST

Data science is the pursuit of objective information, informed by model output. Too often, data scientists today are caught up in the bias of herding towards the most recent innovation in modelling, without a sincere appreciation of the foundational building blocks from mathematics, statistics, and computer science. It is unfortunate that when given a problem to solve, the first answer today (2021) is to use a "random forest" model or an "XG Boost" algorithm without first identifying the nature of the problem. The proceeding chapters expand upon time series (Ch 4), artificial intelligence (AI) (Ch 5) and a framework of using AI (Ch 6). This is not meant to substitute other textbooks, but rather provide the reader with areas that are hardly discussed in the data science profession (at least in my experience). Too often, the realm of time series methods is ignored in many problems in financial services, as we have been accustomed to a logistic regression with panel data, primarily from the studies of experienced data scientists being rooted in actuarial science. With the aid of a colleague, we have created a simple model-building guide below, prior to immersing the reader into some foundation fields of econometrics and AI.

CHAPTER 4

STATISTICAL METHODS USING TIME SERIES DATA

LEARNING OBJECTIVES

After reading this chapter you should be able to:

- Have a basic understanding of time series methods
- See why, how and where time series methods apply to problems in the financial services industry

TIME SERIES METHODS

A set of data points measured at uniform periods of time is referred to as a time series. To model a time series, one needs to be aware of the varying types of seasonality, stationarity, and determinism (level of randomness) present in the series as the presence of each can point towards a different model. Often, in analyzing a time series, one can mistake the presence of chaos in the series as randomness. Chaos can be defined as the irregular behavior of solutions to deterministic equations of motion (Casdagli, 1991). The necessary requirement is that the system of equations be non-linear to generate chaotic solutions as a linear system will necessarily generate a trend in its output. These outputs are often mistaken as random

A Primer on Business Analytics: Perspectives from the Financial Services Industry,
pages 39–52.

time series and are only accurate for a length of time governed by the errors of the initial conditions and the Lyapunov exponent[1] of the system. The following sub-sections discuss the various methods of modelling and explaining time series.

Exponential Smoothing

Exponential smoothing (ES) methods were first developed by Holt (1958). These methods were widely used for business and industrial applications but were often considered a collection of *ad hoc* techniques by academics. Pegels (1969) provided a means of classifying a time series by its trend and seasonal patterns. Both can be linear (additive), non-linear (multiplicative) or neither, giving rise to nine different stochastic models. By graphical illustration of the time series, the classification by Pegels (1969) assists with choosing the best forecasting model to use. Box and Jenkins (1970), *inter alia*, showed that some linear ES forecasts were special cases of ARIMA models. Indeed, the simple ES model can be classified as an ARIMA $(0,1,1)$ model (refer to Definitions page) with no constant term. Snyder (1985) showed that simple ES methods could be considered to originate from an innovation state space model (a model with a single error source). This work prompted later research into state space models and ES methods.

The classification hierarchy by Hyndman et al. (2002) describes the various ES methods. Each ES method can consist of one of five types of trends (none, additive, damped additive, multiplicative and damped multiplicative)[2] and one of three types of seasonality (none, additive or multiplicative). This gives rise to 15 different methods, the most common being that of Simple Exponential Smoothing (which has no trend and no seasonality in the data). Further, the authors provide a theoretical framework that maps ES methods to a state space, showing that they are in the same taxonomy as ARIMA models.

Prediction Intervals

A criticism of ES was that it could not produce prediction intervals for its forecasts. The first analytical approach to this problem by Brown (1963) was to assume that the time series were deterministic functions of time and white noise. If this held true, then a regression model could be used instead of an ES method. This assumption was heavily criticized by Newbold and Bos (1989). The authors note that under the assumption that the time series were deterministic functions of time and white noise, one would: overestimate false signals (Type 1 error), misestimate the probability of the forecast value, misjudge appropriate starting values for the ES method and incorrectly assume that the forecast errors are serially cor-

---

[1] The Lyapunov exponent describes the exponential divergence of the output vectors in a chaotic system.

[2] Where a damped additive trend refers to a time series that has an additive trend that decays over time and a damped multiplicative trend refers to a time series that has a multiplicative trend that decays over time.

related. Other authors since attempted to obtain prediction intervals by examining the equivalence of ES methods and statistical models. In a follow up study, Hyndman et al. (2005) used state space models to derive analytical prediction intervals for 15 ES methods, providing a comprehensive algebraic approach to handling the prediction distribution problem (that an ES model would provide estimates, but not a distribution of forecasts). Given the exploration into ES methods, their more general forms—ARIMA models—are now briefly discussed.

ARIMA Models

Early attempts to study time series in the 20th century began with the idea of a deterministic world, where a change to an initial condition did not result in a different outcome. Yule (1927) provided the first significant contribution of regarding every time series as a stochastic process, where a change in the initial state produces a different outcome. As such, the concept of an autoregressive (AR) model and moving average (MA) model was developed. Wold's decomposition theorem[3] led Kolmogorov (1941) to formulate a solution to the problem of linear forecasting (and later the Kolmogorov Smirnov test for normality). The work of Box and Jenkins (1970) integrated the then existing knowledge on time series and has become a staple addition to any time series course. The Box-Jenkins method is widely used in first testing for stationarity and seasonality, and then proceeding to specify and evaluate the model. With the advent of the computer, autoregressive integrated moving average (ARIMA) models could be developed and used in forecasting discrete time series processes through their univariate forms.

Univariate Models

During the 1960s, the selection of an ARIMA model was largely left to the researcher's judgement, as there was no algorithm available to specify the model correctly. Since then, information criterion techniques have been developed, such as the Akaike Information Criterion (AIC) and the Bayes Information Criterion (BIC). Often, it becomes a task of minimizing these criteria that would result in the best model fit as one would prefer to have estimates as close as possible to actual values to show that the model best describes the data.

There are several methods for estimating the parameters of an ARIMA model, yet they are prone to error when there are large differences in the finite sample properties. Newbold et al. (1994) showed that this difference is significant across the then available software packages and can result in inaccurate forecasts. To overcome the problem, the authors suggest the use of full maximum likelihood estimation[4] to ensure the parameters are statistically consistent. If a time series is

---

[3] Every covariance-stationary time series can be decomposed into the sum of one deterministic and one non-deterministic series.

[4] A method of estimating the parameters of a statistical model, maximum likelihood estimation provides estimates of the mean and variance of a distribution given sample information.

known to follow a univariate ARIMA model, forecasts using disaggregated observations[5] are as good as using aggregated observations under the MSE criterion.

As an alternate to the univariate ARIMA model, Parzen (1982) proposes an ARARMA methodology where the time series is transformed from a long-term memory AR filter to a short-term memory filter. Using data for airline passengers, Parzen (1982) shows that the ARARMA model is a better fit than other more traditional time series models. Meade and Smith (1985) are part of the few authors who test the ARARMA methodology and show that it achieves a significantly low Mean Absolute Percentage Error (MAPE) for longer forecast horizons. While software is available for implementation, these methods are often opaque in that the researcher cannot fully describe the model (it is considered a black box). While there are guidelines for the choice of automatic forecasting methods, Me'Lard and Pasteels (2000) suggest the use of an Expert System as the expert system can more optimally configure the parameters of the model, speeding up the time taken to produce results and quite possibly producing more accurate results.

Non-Linear Models

Compared to the study of linear time series, the development of non-linear time series was still in its infancy as per De Gooijer and Hyndman (2006). The first work in this area is by Volterra (1930) who showed that any continuous non-linear function can be approximated by a finite series with a memory property, later known as a Volterra series. While the probabilistic properties of these models have been studied, little exists in the problem of parameter estimation, model fitting and forecasting. Poskitt and Tremayne (1986) attribute this to the lack of computational power at the time as well as the complexity of the Wiener model itself. While linearity can solve many practical applications, it is often restricted by the existence of complex real-world problems. De Gooijer and Kumar (1992) pointed out one problem with the forecasting ability of non-linear models in that the models made it difficult to obtain analytical expressions for closed-form multi-step ahead forecasts. Researchers could not apply the models (non-analytical) to obtain a finite valued solution (the solution was not closed form). In principle, the Chapman-Kolmogorov relationship (the mapping of joint probability distributions to a stochastic process) can be used to obtain exact least squares multi-step ahead forecasts through integration techniques and currently, these forecasts have been obtained through Monte Carlo simulation or bootstrapping approaches. The latter approach is preferred as it requires no assumptions about the distribution of the error process. Indeed, Clements et al. (2004) concluded that ."... the day is still long off when simple, reliable, and easy to use non-linear model specification, estimation, and forecasting procedures will be readily available." Four such non-linear models are presented below.

---

[5] (Dis)Aggregated observations—Observations combined (removed) from several measurements.

ARCH and GARCH Models

A feature of financial time series is that there are periods of high and low volatility that are often clustered together. This volatility clustering is ideally suited to be modelled by the autoregressive conditional heteroscedastic (ARCH) models of Engle (1982). These models describe the conditional variance as a deterministic (quadratic) function of past returns. As the variance is known at time *t-1*, one-step, and multi-step ahead forecasts can be made. The more general form of ARCH models is given by GARCH models where there are additional dependencies on the lag of the condition variance. These models are fairly like ARIMA models and thus share many statistical properties. Sabbatini and Linton (1998) test a simple GARCH (1,1) model on daily returns of the Swiss market index and find that the out-of-sample forecasts were not accurate. Engle and Ng (1993) point out that asymmetric volatility is often present in financial returns and their conditional variances. Negative (positive) returns are generally associated with an upward (downward) revision of the conditional volatility. As such, researchers have developed GARCH type models to account for this asymmetric volatility.

Long Term Memory Models

When the integration parameter, *d*, in the ARIMA process is fractional and greater than zero, the process is said to have a long-term memory. This implies that the observations that are a long-time span apart have some sort of dependence between them. Stationary long-term memory models or fractionally integrated models (ARFIMA) models have also been developed to allow real values (as opposed to integer values) of the integration parameter. These are thus more apt to modelling long-term dependence as the integration parameter can now take on more values. Souza and Smith (2002) investigated the effect of different frequencies of data on ARFIMA models. They found that the bias in the fractional parameter of a non-aggregated series is influenced by the short-run autoregressive and moving average parameters.

SETAR Models

One of the initial applications of non-linear models to business cycles was shown by Hamilton's (1989) application of Markov Switching techniques. These non-linear models assumed that changes to market phases were governed by an unobserved Markov chain (a process where the next state depends only on the current state). This assumption meant that the exact times a regime (market phase) change occurred were unknown (the *unobserved* part of the assumption), and could only be estimated using probabilities (Hamilton, 1989). Another property of Markov model is that the change (or switch) between regimes is abrupt. In financial markets, it is often difficult to justify this assumption. Further, the changes between an expansionary and contractionary phase of the market cycle need not necessarily be symmetric. It can therefore be inferred that modelling the changes between these regimes of the business cycle can be problematic as they can be either be symmetric or asymmetric and is an issue that STAR models are aptly suited towards. Investors have heterogeneous beliefs, different time horizons and learning speeds (see Harrison & Kreps, 1978 and Bernatzi & Thaler, 1995). These all point to a gradual change in markets as opposed to a more abrupt one. Thus, a new family of models were developed, namely Transition Autoregressive (TAR) models, where they address the issue of a change between regimes. In TAR models, movements are governed by an observed variable and are referred to as Self Exciting TAR (SETAR) models when the observed variable is a lag of the dependent variable. Tong (1983) provided an extensive discussion of Self-Exciting Threshold AR (SETAR) models. These models are piecewise linear models that "partition" the non-linear time series into linear pieces, making estimation of the overall model quicker and less computationally expensive. Other modifications to these models include Threshold VAR (TVAR) models and continuous threshold AR (CTAR) models. While the CTAR models provide highly accurate estimates, they are often impractical due to the higher dimensional integration involved in parameter estimation.

Through examination of the literature on modelling techniques, it emerges that as the accuracy of the model increases, the ability to estimate its parameters and interpret the model itself decreases. This phenomenon is seen in the case of neural networks discussed below. The author states that a small number of outliers in a time series can often mask the simplicity of the series itself. This brings into question the use of macro-economic and micro-economic variables in addition to lagged dependent variables. McMillan (2005) provides international evidence in favor of non-linear modelling of financial markets. An interesting avenue of research is explored by the author linking non-linear behavior of share prices to performance of noise traders, in spirit of the behavioral finance literature of asset prices being dictated by the interaction of noise traders and sophisticated traders. The results show that a non-linear model can capture the effect of noise traders on share prices as well as providing significant gain in forecasting prices out-of-sample for Asian-Pacific economies.

Alagidede and Panagiotidis (2009) provide evidence on testing time series models in several African countries. The authors test each country index for the presence of non-linearity and then proceed to model returns appropriately. Using daily closing prices, the authors find non-linearity in most of their sample, except for South Africa. Bonga-Bonga and Makakabule (2010) use a Smooth Transition Regressive (STR) model is used to investigate the relationship between macro-economic variables and stock returns. The difference between the STAR and STR models is that the former uses lagged values of the independent variable. Whilst the modelling approach is similar, direct comparison of results between STAR and STR models is inappropriate. van Gysen et al. (2013) conduct a comprehensive study of linear and non-linear modelling techniques in forecasting returns on the JSE. The authors find that non-linear methods are favored over their linear counterparts, but less so during turbulent market conditions, such as the financial crisis between 2007 and 2009. Specifically, Markov switching models provide the most accuracy from the family of non-linear models considered.

Neural Networks

While ANNs are adept at forecasting non-linear time series, some have questioned their accuracy. For example, Tkacz (2001) shows that the forecasts of an ANN are outperformed by a naive random walk model. Some attention has also been given to define the border between ANNs and traditional techniques. Balkin and Ord (2000) show that ANNs can work better for high frequency data and also stress the importance of a large dataset to obtain more accurate training and forecasts of the ANN. Qi (2001) observed that an ANN is more likely to outperform other methods when the input data is as current as possible and using a recursive modelling procedure. Swanson and White (1997) show that a simple feed-forward ANN with a single hidden layer offers a highly useful and flexible alternative to a linear model, particularly in multi-step ahead forecasts, as the linear model needs to be specified in advance whenever new information becomes available over an extended time period. A comparison between ANNs and an ARIMA model is given by Ghiassi et al. (2005). They find their dynamic ANN performs significantly better than a traditional ARIMA model based on MSE statistics and the Morgan-Granger-Newbold test for autocorrelation between the positive and negative sum of the error terms.

Given the array of time-series based models to choose from, the researcher must also be cognizant of the inputs to the model. Indeed, choosing appropriate inputs are as important as choosing the correct functional model form.

CASE STUDY

Time Series Analysis and Forecasting: Novel Business Perspectives
Time series forecasting is hardly a new problem in data science and statistics. The term is self-explanatory and has been on business analysts' agenda for decades now: The very first practices of time series analysis and forecasting trace back to the early 1920s.

The underlying idea of time series forecasting is to look at historical data from the time perspective, define the patterns, and yield short or long-term predictions on how— considering the captured patterns—target variables will change in the future. The use cases for this approach are numerous, ranging from sales and inventory predictions to highly specialized scientific works on bacterial ecosystems.

Although an intern analyst today can work with time series in Excel, the growth of computing power and data tools allows for leveraging time series for much more complex problems than before to achieve higher prediction accuracy.

Time Series Problems

Many machine-learning and data-mining tasks operate with datasets that have a single slice of time or don't consider the time aspect at all. Natural language processing, image or sound recognition, and numerous classification and regression problems can be solved without time variables at all. For example, the sound recognition solution that we worked with entailed capturing specific teeth grinding sounds of patients as they slept. So, we weren't interested in how these sounds change over time, but rather how to distinguish them from ambient sounds.

Time series problems, on the other hand, are always time-dependent and we usually look at four main components: seasonality, trends, cycles, and irregular components.

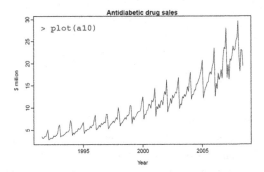

Source: Forecasting: Principles & Practice, Rob J Hyndman, 2014

Trends and seasonality are clearly visible

The graph above is a clear example of how trends and seasons work.

Trends. The trend component describes how the variable—drug sales in this case—changes over long periods of time. We see that the sales revenues of antidiabetic drugs have substantially increased during the period from the 1990s to 2010s.

Seasons. The seasonal component showcases each year's wave-like changes in sales patterns. Sales were increasing and decreasing seasonally. Seasonal series can be tied to any time measurement. We can consider monthly or quarterly patterns for sales in midsize or small eCommerce, or track micro interactions across a day.

Cycles. Cycles are long-term patterns that have a wave form and recurring nature similar to seasonal patterns but with variable length. For example, business cycles have recognizable elements of growth, recession, and recovery. But the cycles themselves stretch in time differently for a given country throughout its history.

Irregularities. Irregular components appear due to unexpected events, like cataclysms, or are simply representative of noise in the data.

Today, time series problems are usually solved by conventional statistical (e.g. ARIMA) and machine learning methods, including artificial neural networks (ANN), support vector machine (SVM), and some others. While these approaches have proved their efficiency, the tasks, their scope, and our abilities to solve the problems change. And the mere set of use cases for time series today has a potential to be expanded. As statistics step into the era of big data processing, the Internet of Things providing limitless trackable devices, and social media analysis, analysts look for new approaches to handle this data and convert it into predictions.

So, let's survey the main things that are happening in the field.

Methods to Combat Non-Stationary Data
Prediction is very difficult, especially if it's about the future.
Nils Bohr, Nobel laureate in Physics

Traditional forecasting methods strive to bring stationarity into time series, i.e. make a number of statistical properties repeat constantly over time. Raw data doesn't usually provide enough stationarity to yield confident predictions. For instance, to the graph of antidiabetic drug sales above, we must apply multiple mathematical transformations to render non-stationary time series at least approximately stationary. Then we'll be able to find patterns and make predictions that are more accurate than coin tossing, which is right in 50 percent of cases.

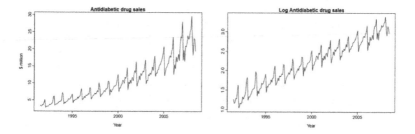

Source: Forecasting: Principles & Practice, Rob J Hyndman, 2014

Bringing Stationarity to Data
But time series in some fields are very resistant to our efforts as there are too many irregular factors that impact changes. Look at travel disruptions, especially those that happen during political unrest and the dangers of terrorism. Traveler streams change, destinations change, and airlines are adjusting their prices differently making year-old observations nearly obsolete. Or crude oil prices, which are critical to predict for players across many industries, haven't permitted us to build time series algorithms that would be precise enough.

Traditional Machine Learning Methods
The traditional machine learning approach is to split an available historic dataset into two or three smaller sets to train a model and to further validate its performance against data that a machine hasn't seen before. If we apply machine learning without the time series factor, a data scientist can choose the most relevant records from the available data and fit the model to them, leaving noisy and inconsistent records behind.

In time series, the main difference is that a data scientist needs to use a validation set that exactly follows a training set on the time axis to see whether the trained model is good enough. The problem with non-stationary records is that data in the training set might not be homogeneous to the testing set, as time series properties substantially change over the period that training and validation sets cover.

Stream Learning Approach

Here's when we can use the stream learning technique. Stream learning suggests incremental changes to the algorithm—basically, its re-training. As a new record or a small set of them comes in, it updates the model instead of processing a whole set of data. This approach requires the understanding of two main things:

Data Horizon

How many new training instances are needed to update the model? For example, Shuang Gao and Yalin Lei from the China University of Geosciences recently applied stream learning to increase prediction accuracy in such non-stationary time series as crude oil prices mentioned above. They've set the data horizon as small as possible so that every update on the oil prices immediately updates the algorithm.

Data Obsolescence

How long does it take to start considering historic data or some of its elements irrelevant? The answer to this question may be quite tricky as it requires a share of assumptions based on domain expertise, basically, an understanding of how the market you work with changes and how many non-stationary factors bombard it. If your eCommerce business has significantly grown since last year both in terms of customer base and product variety, the data of the same quarter of the previous year may be considered obsolete. On the other hand, if the country experiences economic recession the new short-term data may be less enlightening than that of the previous recession.

While crude oil forecasts based on stream learning eventually perform better than conventional methods, they still show results that are only slightly better than a flipped coin does and stay in a ballpark of 60 percent confidence. They are also more complicated in development, deployment, and require prior business analysis to figure out data horizon and obsolescence.

Ensemble Methods

Another way to struggle with non-stationarity is ensemble models. Ensembling uses multiple machine learning and data mining methods to further combine their results and increase predictive accuracy. The technique has nothing to do with new approaches in data science, but it has critical meaning in terms of business decisions related to data science initiatives.

Basically, while building robust forecasting is expensive and time-consuming, it doesn't narrow down to making and validating one or two models with further choosing of the best performer. In terms of time series, non-stationary components—like different durations of cycles, low weather predictability, and other irregular events that have an impact across multiple industries—make things even harder.

This was the problem for the Google team that was building time series forecasting infrastructure to analyze business dynamics of their search engine and YouTube with further disaggregating these forecasts for regions and small-time series like days and weeks. With Google engineers recently disclosing their approach, it became clear that even the Mount Olympus of AI-driven technologies chooses simpler methods over complex ones. They don't use stream learning yet and settle for ensemble methods. But the main point that they express is that you need as many methods as possible to get the best results:

> So, what models do we include in our ensemble? Pretty much any reasonable model we can get our hands on! Specific models include variants on many well-known approaches, such as the Bass Diffusion Model, the Theta Model, Logistic models, bsts, STL, Holt-Winters and other Exponential Smoothing models, Seasonal and other ARIMA-based models, Year-over-Year growth models, custom models, and more.
>
> —*Eric Tassone and Farzan Rohani*

By averaging the forecast of many models that perform differently in different time series situations, they achieved better predictability than they could with a single model. While some models work better with their specific non-stationary data, others shine in theirs. The average that they yield acts like an expert opinion and turns out to be very precise.

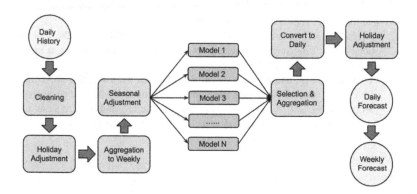

Source: Our quest for robust time series forecasting at scale, Eric Tassone and Farzan Rohani, 2017, Forecast procedure in Google

However, the authors of the post note that this approach may be the best one for their specific situation. Google services stretch across many countries where different factors like electricity, internet speed, user working cycles are adding too many non-stationary patterns. So, if you aren't operating with a multitude of locations or a large set of varying data sources, ensemble models may not be for you. But if you track time series patterns across countries or business units in different regions it might be the best fit.

Automation of Time Series Forecasting

A couple of months ago we published overview of MLaaS platforms for semi and fully automated machine learning tasks that can be approached by organizations with limited access to data science and analytics talent.

The problem with automation in prediction and machine learning operations is that the technologies are still in their infancy. Fully automated solutions suffer from the lack of flexibility as they perform many operations under the hood and can either do straightforward and general tasks (like objects recognition on pictures) or fail to capture business specifics. On the other hand, hiring full-blown data science teams may be cost-sensitive in the early stages of your analytics initiative. A happy medium here are instruments like TensorFlow, that still require some engineering talent on board but provide enough automation and convenient tools to avoid reinventing the wheel.

Facebook's Prophet

The great contributor to the operationalization of time series prediction is Prophet, a new open-source product from Facebook with an epic name. Facebook has been quite generous in open sourcing the tools they use, remember React Native that was released for public use in 2013. But this time they give away a pretty task-specific package.

Prophet is positioned as "Forecasting at Scale," which according to the authors means mainly 3 things:

1. A broad variety of people can use the package. Potential users are both data scientists and people who have the domain knowledge to configure data sources and integrate Prophet into their analytics infrastructures.
2. A broad variety of problems can be addressed. Facebook used the tool for social media time series forecasting, but the model is configurable to match various business circumstances.
3. Performance evaluation is automated. Here comes the sweetest part. Evaluation and a number of surface problems are automated and human analysts just have to visually inspect forecasts, do the modeling, and react to situations when the machine thinks that forecasts have a high error probability.

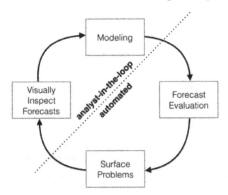

Source: Forecasting at Scale, Sean J. Taylor and Benjamin Letham, 2017

Modeling, in this case, means that analysts use their domain knowledge and external data to tweak the work of Prophet. For instance, you can input market size data or other capacities information to let the algorithm consider these factors and adjust to them. As you know when you are going to roll out some game-changing updates, like a site redesign or some mind-blowing feature, you can also signal the algorithm about these. And eventually, you can define the relevant scale of seasonality and even add holidays as recurring patterns in your time series. All retailers know how different the Black Friday or Christmas are from the rest of the year.

Twitter and Microsoft
Back in 2013, a social media giant, Twitter, released their time series package. It's a bit off-topic because their tool is aimed at anomaly detection and is called... AnomalyDetection. It's also automatic and isn't aimed at social media only but extends to any field where time series analysis is applied, especially when you monitor many series for different products, stores, or markets. While AnomalyDetection doesn't forecast the future, it helps to automatically detect time-dependent anomalies. This is very helpful in distributed architectures with large traffic to spot spammers, bots, or simply explore what kinds of events impact your business performance in different locations. Have you accounted for all weird holidays?

The reason we're mentioning Twitter here is that both Prophet and AnomalyDetection are representatives of the emerging automation trend in the time series field. Pretty soon these operations are going to become more affordable and potentially move to the popular cloud infrastructures. For example, Microsoft recently rolled out its Azure Time Series Insights for IoT that doesn't seem to add the prediction capacity yet but already provides data streaming from devices and allows for anomaly detection.

Time Series Forecasting as a Sales and UX Lever
There has always been a precise distinction between machine learning tasks that you solve to run internal analytics and customer-facing ML-based applications. Good examples of the latter are facial recognition apps, neural networks to process images, or recommendation engines in online content services.

Internal analytics have usually been employed to gain business insights. But things get the new perspective as giving away some prediction results, especially those that relate to time series seems a great opportunity for improving and personalizing the user experience.

One of those cases is our client Fareboom.com. Fareboom is a flight-booking service that succeeds in finding the lowest air fares possible for its customers. The problem with airfares is that they change rapidly and without obvious reasons. Unless you're buying tickets right before a trip, future pricing information would be advantageous. A great UX solution was to predict whether the prices are going to drop or increase in the near or distant future and give this information to customers. This encourages customer making return and makes Fareboom their go-to platform for optimizing their travel budgets.

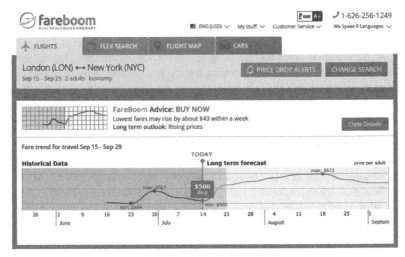

Source: Fareboom.com

The engine has 75 percent confidence that the fares will rise soon

Giving away at least some of your analytics is a particularly good strategy for the travel industry and generally all businesses that connect people with end-service providers. If you have seasonal or trending data on the hotels that people enjoy during Christmas, why not turn it into recommendations?

The Main Trend
Both time series automation and the growth of available data from endpoint devices define the main trend in time series forecasting. Analytics are becoming increasingly more affordable and eventually more critical for business success. Not only can we track business progress, but also, we can capture very specific—non-stationary and sometimes—time dependent events that were missing before. And the emerging power of intermediary services contributes to this availability trend.

The main concern today's executives should be defining an analytics strategy, whether it's going to be customer-facing or internal, and leading the initiative.

https://www.altexsoft.com/blog/business/time-series-analysis-and-forecasting-novel-business-perspectives/

QUESTIONS

1. Under what circumstances should one use a model appropriate for time series data?
2. How does one choose the optimal time series model?
3. How relevant are time series models in financial services? Provide examples where they are and are not.

CHAPTER 5

ARTIFICIAL INTELLIGENCE

Over the course of human evolution, we have developed increasingly sophisticated tools to serve a multitude of purposes. The advent of the digital computer provided a means of performing numeric and symbolic manipulations at a greater speed than ourselves. Penrose (1998) pointed out that most humans are quite content with a machine being able to do physical, labor-intensive tasks, some of which we are incapable of (such as flying). The realm of artificial intelligence (AI) is directed toward building such a machine. Akrimi et al. (2013) define artificial intelligence as the science of mimicking human mental faculties in a computer. The goal of AI is to construct a machine that can, at the very least, mimic human behavior. On the path to achieving this goal, a variety of useful computing tools have been developed. These tools enable more effective problem solving as well as consideration of problems that previously did not exist (or at least were not fully understood).

The tools of AI can be categorized into: Knowledge based systems (KBS) where these models use words and symbols and Computational Intelligence (CI) that uses numerical techniques.

KBS type tools include rule-based, model-based, frame-based, and case-based reasoning (discussed later). As these tools use words and symbols, their output can be easily understood. While successful, their application to a variety of problems becomes limited, as they are only able to handle problems that are explicitly defined. In contrast, CI type tools are useful at dealing with problems that are

A Primer on Business Analytics: Perspectives from the Financial Services Industry,
pages 53–79.
Copyright © 2022 by Information Age Publishing

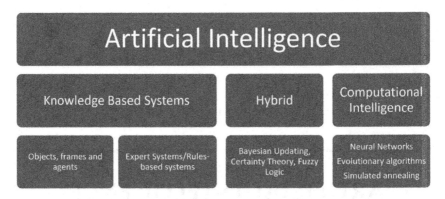

FIGURE 5.1.   Representation of the Fields Within AI (adapted from Akrimi et al., 2013)

not always explicitly defined where they learn by experience and observation. Knowledge is represented by numbers rather than words and can be adjusted to boost the accuracy of the output. Neural networks, search algorithms and optimization algorithms are part of CI tools. The field of AI are categorized as per Figure 5.1, where KBS software uses words and symbols in solving problems in contrast to CI software that uses numerical techniques. The overlap between these two areas contains techniques from Bayesian probability and fuzzy logic[1]. Each area is discussed in the subsequent sections below.

LEARNING OBJECTIVES

After reading this chapter you should be able to:

- Understand the broad scope of machine learning and computational intelligence.
- Appreciate the history of artificial intelligence.
- Appreciate that data science/artificial intelligence/machine learning is not "new".
- Have basic knowledge of the different types of learning and supervision techniques in the field of computational intelligence.

KNOWLEDGE BASED AND EXPERT SYSTEMS

The difference between a KBS and a conventional computing program lies in its structure. In a conventional program, domain knowledge is combined with the

---

[1] A form of many-valued logic that approximates reasoning rather than providing a fixed and exact form.

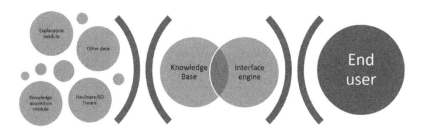

FIGURE 5.2. Representation of an Expert System (adapted from Akrimi et al., 2013)

software for controlling its application. In a KBS, the two roles are explicitly separated into a knowledge module and a control module, often called an inference engine as seen in Figure 5.2. Within the knowledge base, the programmer codes information about the problem to be solved. This is often declarative in that there are facts, rules, and relationships without any concern about how or when these should be applied. Details of the application are stored in the inference engine that is often steered by the programmer. This is referred to as metaknowledge (knowledge about knowledge). In the most complex case, the inference engine can contain metaknowledge as well. As the knowledge is represented explicitly in the knowledge base, it can be updated with ease by outside users without any *a priori* experience about the KBS itself.

Expert systems are a type of KBS designed to embody expertise in a specialized domain. They act as a human expert in that they are consulted when the outside user describes a problem (or rather symptoms of a problem) that is then diagnosed by the expert system. Often, the expert system needs to offer certain justifications for its current line of inquiry as well as explaining its reasoning to arrive at a conclusion. This is housed within the explanation module in Figure 5.2. The amount of knowledge that can be represented in rules is somewhat limited when modelling real world systems. Frames provide flexibility in this regard— they can model complex systems allowing for flexible and versatile rules. For example, in the medical profession, the link between symptoms and a diagnosis is often blurred. The use of case-based reasoning is useful in these scenarios, as the system will draw on experience and observation to make an informed decision. A short digression on the technical aspects of storing knowledge is now considered.

FRAME BASED SYSTEMS

Frames (objects) are data structures that represent and organize knowledge. Like object-oriented systems (a related group of data and procedures), frame-based systems contain classes, instances, and inheritance. For example, the class of *de-*

Degree		
Type	Value: Character	
	Range = (Undergraduate, Postgraduate)	
Discipline	Value: Character	
	Range = (Science, Commerce, Medicine, Humanities, Engineering)	
Length	Value: Integer	
	Range = 1,...,8	

slots { ... } *facets*

FIGURE 5.3. Representation of a Facet (Source: The Author)

gree can be defined along with subclasses of *undergraduate* and *postgraduate.* Characteristics of the class *degree* are inherited by its subclasses so that only information specific to a subclass is declared and stored. Specific instances of classes can then be declared, for example, "*I am studying towards a postgraduate degree.*" This instance inherits information from the subclass of *postgraduate degree* that in turn inherits information from the class *degree.*

The attributes of a frame are also known as slots, into which values can be inserted. To extend the above example, an attribute of number of years of study can be inserted into the frame. The slot can be loaded with a default value or it may be locally defined. Further, slots can hold text, numeric, procedures or even another frame. If different values are placed into the same slot, these become known as facets and are shown in Figure 5.3.

Fulton and Pepe (1990) highlight three inadequacies of a pure rule-based system. First, building a complete rule set is a large task to accomplish; second, there is uncertainty arising from whether the output can be believable and third, maintaining the rules is a complex task because of the interdependencies between them. Based on these shortcomings, the authors argue for a model-based approach. In model-based reasoning, the symptom-cause pairs of information are generated by applying the underlying principles to the model. This contrasts with rule-based reasoning where the pairs are stored in the model itself. Given this framework, the methods of populating the knowledge attributes are now discussed.

LEARNING

If we assume that knowledge is not readily available or explicitly expressed, then it remains a task of acquiring said knowledge for the efficient functioning of the system. Two approaches for learning (knowledge acquisition) have been used in the literature, namely symbolic learning, and numeric learning. Symbolic learning describes systems that learn and modify rules, facts and relationships based on information expressed as words or symbols. Simply, symbolic learning allows systems to create their own knowledge base. Numeric learning describes systems that create their own knowledge base from numerical methods. Such learning techniques include neural networks, search algorithms and optimization algorithms. The learning system itself usually has feedback on its performance. The source of the feedback is usually the external environment (the reaction of the environment to an output or decision is usually sufficient to indicate whether the output or decision was correct). In this scenario, where there is a guide or teacher to determine whether the output was correct, the learning system is categorized as supervised learning.

Forms of supervised learning include:

1. Rote learning (colloquially referred to as "parrot learning"), where the system receives information on correct decisions and when an incorrect decision is reached, the decision is overridden by the correct decision.
2. Learning from advice, where the system is given general advice on how the decision should be reached and the system determines by itself how it can reach this decision.
3. Learning by induction, where the system is presented with sets of example data, given the correct decisions and it is left to refine its rules and relationships to handle new examples.
4. Learning by analogy, where the system is told the correct decision to a similar, yet not identical task. The system is then left to adapt its previous decision to generate a new rule to match the correct decision.
5. Explanation-based learning (EBL), where the system analyses a set of example solutions and outcomes to determine why one solution was successful over another. EBL is incorporated into a well-known computer program (known as *PRODIGY*) to solve general purpose problems (Minton et al., 1989).
6. Case-based reasoning (CBR), where any case is filed away with the decision and the system cross references the current case against stored cases.
7. Unsupervised learning, where the explorative system continuously searches for patterns and relationships in the data. Examples of unsupervised learning include data mining and cluster analysis.

As one progresses through the points above, the ability of the teacher becomes increasingly important to the success of the system output. The most common used method is cased-based reasoning and is discussed in more detail. A characteristic of human intelligence is the ability to recall prior experiences whenever a new problem arises. Case-based reasoning personifies this description. According to Riesbeck and Schank (1989), a cased-based reasoner solves new problems by adapting solutions that were used to solve old problems. Aamodt and Plaza (1994) propose that CBR be described in a four-stage cycle. The CBR will (1) retrieve the most similar case(s); (2) reprocess the case(s) to attempt to solve the problem; (3) revise the proposed solution if necessary; and (4) retain the new solution as part of a new case. This approach approximates the human experience to reasoning quite well. In practice, CBR is used in a semi-supervised environment, where the researcher can intervene if necessary. These forms of learning apply to both KBS and CI software, the latter of which is discussed below.

COMPUTATIONAL INTELLIGENCE

The invention of machine learning has made a profound impact in pushing computer science and AI a step closer to building a thinking machine. Machine learning enables a computer program to analyze a large dataset and decide on information most relevant to the problem it is faced with. This information (whether clustered, sorted or classified) can then be used to make predictions with greater speed and accuracy. These machine learning techniques have been collected into a freely available software package called WEKA (Waikato Environment for Knowledge Analysis). WEKA can provide researchers with several standard Machine Learning (ML) techniques to solve real world problems. Figure 5.4 shows the hierarchy of neural network architectures. ANNs can be categorized based on learning and supervision. In the case of supervised learning, the network is presented with examples of which it attempts to match. These networks can accommodate time series and cross-sectional data and differ only in the flow of data from the input layer to the output layer—in a feed forward network, data is fed only in one direction, that of from the input layer to the output layer. In contrast, a recurrent network has a bi-directional flow of data between the input, hidden and output layers. Two examples of unsupervised learning would be Self Organizing Maps (SOMS), which is a form of clustering; and Adaptive Resonance Theory.

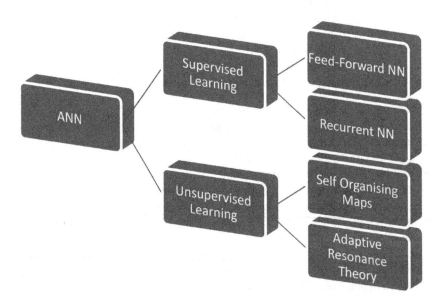

FIGURE 5.4.   Classification Tree of ANNs (Source: The Author)

SUPERVISED LEARNING TECHNIQUES

Once preliminary testing is completed on the data set, the classifier (mapping from unlabeled instances to classes) is available for use. This can be achieved by one of three methods—splitting the dataset into a training and validation set: cross validation and a leave-one-out method. In the cross-validation technique, the training set is divided into mutually exclusive and equally sized subsets. The average error rate for each subset is therefore considered the error rate of the classifier. In the leave-one-out method, all except one data subset is used in the process. This method is computationally more expensive but useful when the most accurate estimate of the error rate is required. If the error rate evaluation is unsatisfactory, then the researcher returns to the problem and dataset to investigate causes of non-performance. Often, the cause can be the size of the dataset, the dimensionality being too high, an inappropriate classifier algorithm was used, or the dataset could be imbalanced[2] (Japkowicz & Stephen, 2002).

Supervised ML algorithms are usually compared via statistical tests. If there is a sufficiently large data set, then a sample set of size N can be used to run two different algorithms. The difference in accuracy between these two samples is validated via a Student's t-test. While this test can produce two types of errors (Type I error or Type II error), it is an estimate of whether there is a difference in the accuracy of two classifiers. In practice however, as there is usually only one dataset of size N, the dataset is split into subsets and the test is performed accordingly. Unfortunately, this causes a problem of non-independence in the sample and can significantly raise the Type I error of incorrectly rejecting the null hypothesis. Bouckaert (2003) suggests that the sampling be repeated several times with different random partitions—in effect the size of the sub-sample is randomly chosen, and the tests are performed on "differing" sample sizes. This would ensure that the results obtained are robust across the sample and not an anomaly found in one sub-sample. Two popular supervised techniques are now discussed, namely that of Support Vector Machines and Decision Trees. For a survey of techniques, the reader is directed to Kotsiantis et al. (2007).

Support Vector Machine (SVM)

An SVM is a discriminative classifier that learns the decision surface through a process of discrimination and with good generalization characteristics. Informally, an SVM will separate the initial data set into two or more distinct groups and then assign new examples to one of those groups. The result can be shown graphically with each group being represented as a cluster. SVMs are used widely in semantic classification and learning tasks. Training an SVM involves optimization of a convex cost function. These algorithms are most referred to as Kernel Methods as they use kernel substitution to solve a multitude of learning and clas-

---

[2] An imbalanced dataset has several categories of variables, not all of which are equally represented.

sification problems (Cristianini & Shawe-Taylor, 2000). The advantages of an SVM lie in its good generalization capability—they can easily distribute data in its feature space and missing data does not affect the quality of output. Further, these algorithms are enhanced through statistical learning in that the bounds of the generalization error can be obtained. Like how the error term from a regression is calculated, so too can the SVM produce a generalization error between where the example should truly be placed and where most data points with similar characteristics are placed on a graph. One possible disadvantage with the use of an SVM is that the learning algorithm (the process of classifying examples to a distinct group) is not always perfectly visible. As a result, an alternate technique, that of a Decision Tree, can be used.

Decision Trees

Decision trees (Figure 5.5) classify instances by sorting them based on feature values. Each node in a tree represents a feature in an instance that needs to be classified and each branch represents a value that the node can assume. Instances are classified starting at the root node and are sorted based on their feature values. Similar to an SVM, decision trees provide a means of grouping data, albeit with a greater level of interpretation—one can easily see the decisions taken to arrive at grouping a particular data point in a decision tree, whereas in an SVM, the learning algorithm is not always apparent.

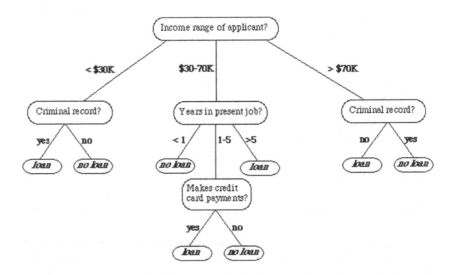

FIGURE 5.5. A decision tree (Source: https://towardsdatascience.com/what-is-a-decision-tree-22975f00f3e1)

Methods such as information gain and the Gini coefficient can be used to find the feature that best divides the training data at the root node of the tree. A decision tree, *h*, is said to overfit the training data if another tree *h'* exists that has a larger error than *h* when tested on the training data, but a smaller error than *h* when tested on the entire dataset. To avoid overfitting, the researcher can stop the training algorithm before it reaches a point where it perfectly fits the training data or prune the induced decision tree. If two trees have the same prediction accuracy, then the one would fewer leaves is preferred. Breslow and Aha (1997), in a survey of tree simplification methods, conclude that pre-pruning is the easiest way to avoid overfitting. While this may be true, Elomaa (1999) concludes that there is no single best pruning method. While a non-trivial termination criterion can be applied to the tree, decision tree classifiers usually employ post-pruning techniques that evaluate the performance of the tree as they are pruned using a validation set. A node can be removed and assigned the most common class of the training instances that are sorted to it. Thus, the accuracy of a decision tree in correctly classifying data into reasonable clusters rests (to a large extent) on the abilities of the researcher to prune nodes that overfit the data. In contrast, an SVM does not require as much input from the researcher regarding post-fitting processes.

Discussion on Techniques

As the choice of algorithm depends on the task at hand and the researcher's preferences, a summary of techniques is presented here. SVMs and neural networks tend to perform better when dealing with multidimensional problems with continuous features. Indeed, these techniques are suited for problems where multicollinearity is present as well as non-linearity. In contrast, logic-based systems perform better with discrete or categorical features. SVMs and ANNs require large samples in order to achieve high prediction accuracy and make use of an error-correcting output coding (ECOC) approach to reduce a multiclass problem to a set of multiple binary classification problems—a similar concept to reducing the dimensionality of input data (Crammer & Singer, 2002). Naive Bayes classifiers usually have a high bias, as they assume that the dataset can be summarized by a single probability distribution. In contrast, high-decision algorithms such as decision trees, ANNs and SVMs can be more useful, but also more prone to overfitting. Logic based algorithms are easy to interpret in contrast to ANNs and SVMs as well as being more transparent to the researcher. This is summarized in Table 5.1. For each characteristic, the ability of the selected AI techniques is rated between 1 (poor) and 5 (exceptional). For example, Support Vector Machines have the highest accuracy in general, but the lowest speed in learning. Neural networks have the highest speed of classifying data but poor explanatory power.

When faced with the decision of choosing the best algorithm, the simplest approach is to determine which is the most accurate. Alternatively, one can also combine approaches to yield surprisingly more accurate predictions. Often, su-

TABLE 5.1. Summary of Advantages and Disadvantages of AI Techniques (Kotsiantis et al., 2007)

	Decision Trees	Neural Networks	Naïve Bayes	ANN	SVM	Rule-Learners
Accuracy in general	2	3	1	2	4	2
Speed of learning with respect to number of attributes and the number of instances	3	1	4	4	1	2
Speed of classification	4	4	4	1	4	4
Tolerance to missing values	3	1	4	1	2	2
Tolerance to redundant attributes	3	1	2	2	4	2
Tolerance to highly interdependent attributes	2	2	1	2	3	2
Dealing with discrete, binary, or continuous attributes	4	3^1	3^2	3^3	2^1	3^3
Tolerance to noise	2	1	3	3	2	2
Dealing with danger of overfitting	2	1	3	3	2	2
Attempts for incremental learning	2	3	4	4	2	1
Explanation ability, transparency of knowledge or classification	4	1	4	2	1	4
Model parameter handling	3	1	4	3	1	3

Notes: [1] not discrete; [2] not continuous; [3] not directly discrete

pervised techniques are combined with their counterparts to produce more accurate results.

UNSUPERVISED LEARNING TECHNIQUES

In contrast to supervised or reinforced learning, unsupervised learning refers to a set of algorithms that attempt to group data into sizeable, relevant groups based on data points with similar characteristics—there is no objective function to fit the data to. These techniques do not rely on minimizing an error term and are thus prone to overfitting the data. Quite contrary to the name, these techniques place more emphasis on the evaluation of the output model by the researcher. Two techniques are discussed here—genetic programming and self-organizing maps.

Genetic Programming

Genetic Programming (GP) is a form of artificial intelligence that mimics the processes observed in natural evolution; and was first introduced by Koza (1992) as a modification to genetic algorithms. Mathematically, GP is a non-linear search procedure used for optimization problems, which are commonly expressed as decision trees. The term, GP, encompasses five key areas: population, evaluation, selection, crossover, and mutation.

A population of random solutions, called the first generation, is produced. Most of these solutions will be a poor match to the output data as defined by the output criteria. However, some will meet the criteria purely by chance. The population will then evolve over a series of generations to better match the output data. Each evolution is created by cross-over or mutation of the approved solutions. In biological terms, the first generation (adult) solutions that passed the output criteria reproduce the subsequent generation (children). A cross-over mixes sub-trees of the parent population, whereas a mutation will replace the sub-tree with a new, randomly generated sub-tree (Koza, 1992). Individual solutions with a good fit to the criteria are more likely to survive and reproduce than individuals with a low fit. The GP process continues until either a solution is found, or a fixed number of generations have been reached (determined by the researcher). Thus, the GP will search the solution space, with more evolved generations being more adept at finding a solution. While GP is not necessarily better than the traditional linear programming methods, it is more efficient at solving unconventional problems.

Some applications of GP have been found in economics and finance and are discussed here. While it may seem that too much detail is provided for these studies, these studies lend support in building a case for the use of artificial intelligence in solving financial problems. For example, Kaboudan (1999) uses GP to measure share price predictability. A cause of uncertainty in a series can be due to the series itself being a stochastic process, in which cases there is no model to fit the data generating process, or a model could exist, but the universe of explanatory variables is near infinite. Kaboudan (1999) argues that GP can be used to investigate this problem in stock return data and isolate the unpredictable process of the series. This would thereby eliminate much of the exploration into explanatory variables that have no influence on the series. The author also notes that if a series is found unpredictable via GP, it does not necessarily imply that the series is stochastic as the choice of algorithm in GP could very well be ill suited for the task at hand. Thus, the author proposes a two-stage procedure when utilizing GP. The first where predictability is measured, relevant variables are identified and the structure of the data generating process emerges. The second determines the data generating process itself. Results from the author's investigation show that if the computed value of the introduced measure approaches zero, the data is random or unpredictable. Analyzing high frequency trading data (price changes per minute or half an hour), the author finds differing results per stock analyzed. In general, it is concluded that if a series' data generating process is a combination of linear and non-linear or linear, non-linear, and stochastic, then the predictability of the series decreases significantly.

GP may also be used to generate implications of the behavior of market participants. Lensburg (1999) explores this area. At the time of writing, there was an influx of techniques from biology to economics; the most noted being that of using genetic programming to model artificially intelligent agents that are boundedly rational. Specifically, GP could well be suited to model the evolution of games (the interaction of agents), where more than one Nash (optimum) equilibrium exists. As a multiple equilibrium game does not imply rationality on its agents, the use of GP tests this hypothesis. Lensburg (1999) considers a case where the agents face Knightian uncertainty—the agents have no *a priori* beliefs about the returns of the game and no learning rule can be used to obtain such beliefs. The author finds that when investors receive the same information about an unknown probability distribution, those investors behave as expected utility maximisers with Bayesian learning; a surprising result given that the agents do not maximize their utility levels and they do not have access to any means of estimating the parameters of an unknown probability distribution.

Sullivan et al. (1999) use GP in trading strategies. The authors argue that studies that test the EMH using technical analysis are subject to data mining and predisposed to rejecting the EMH. When examining the effectiveness of trading rules, one needs to be cautious of data snooping (the use of a given set of data multiple times for the purposes of inference or model selection). Indeed, Brock et al. (1992) state that given the multitude of trading rules, it is quite possible that one would work purely by chance. These authors also acknowledge the effect of data snooping and, as future research, state that one should compute the effectiveness of all trading rules, given that the results of some rules are dependent on others. Thus, Sullivan *et al.* (1999) expand on this concept and use GP to examine the effectiveness of trading rules. Often, the trading rule chosen is done so based on prior performance. It is difficult to argue that these rules became popular based on their *ex-post* performance. Therefore, these trading rules must be expected to perform well at some historical point in time. Studying the efficacy of the trading rule on historical data will most likely result in a positive outcome, leading to a premature rejection of the EMH. Over the 100-year sample period, the authors investigate the efficacy of nearly 8000 trading rules (after costs) in beating the market index. They find that the probability of such occurring is 12%, concluding that technical analysis was of little relevance during their sample period.

The dynamics of exchange rates has not received much attention in the past, with many authors showing no true evidence on exchange rate predictability. Given the advances in forecasting techniques, Alvarez-Diaz and Alvarez (2005) combine GP and ANNs to forecast exchange rates. Given that the exchange rate may be a function of linear and stochastic processes, it is quite a complex task to disentangle the effects of complicated relationships between potential explanatory variables. This may incorrectly result in an interpretation of randomness when the series is chaotic and non-linear. The authors combine AI techniques to predict the evolution of the Japanese Yen and Pound Sterling against the U.S. Dollar. Their results show that even with the more sophisticated tools used, there is no significant improvement in forecasting ability of the above exchange rates. They offer three reasons for this result. First, there may exist weak non-linear structures in the exchange rates that do not contribute significantly to the forecasts. Second, there exists a predictable non-linear component that their research design did not expose. Last, there is a greater level of complexity than previously expected in the exchange rate dynamics, requiring a larger sample period and size.

Self-Organizing Maps

The Self-Organizing Map of Kohonen (1990) is an artificial neural network in which the cells become specifically attuned to various input signal patterns or classes of patterns through unsupervised learning. In the basic SOM, only one cell or local group of cells at a time gives the active response to a current input. The location of the responses become ordered and then correspond to a particular domain of input signal patterns, where cells of the higher valued response are prioritized over lower valued response cells. For example, consider a classroom of students, with desks neatly arranged in rows and columns. When the class is asked a question by the teacher, the student first to respond is the most knowledgeable about that question. As new questions, not necessarily related to each other, are asked, it is plausible that a different student would answer. Thus, one can consider each responding student to be the most knowledgeable about a certain area of knowledge. In effect, this is how a SOM is constructed. Data are presented to the cells of the network and those cells that respond quicker (or more accurately) are considered knowledgeable about the input data. Thus, once each example has been presented to the network, there would exist clusters in the SOM that correspond to data with similar characteristics.

The SOM was developed as an alternative to more traditional ANN architectures to account for unsupervised learning and an alternative for decision trees. While its development has led to vast technical improvements, it has not developed much in a biological sense. Nonetheless, the learning process is natural and can be likened somewhat to brain activity (as per the example discussed above, each student would process the question and answer it they believe their answer is correct). SOMs have been used in several practical settings to solve classification problems. The spatial segmentation ability of a SOM enables it to have a high degree of efficiency in classifying complex problems. While the speed of learning in a SOM can be increased significantly and quite easily, the larger the map becomes, the more hierarchical systems are favored. SOMs are preferred when there are departures from the generic characteristics (anomalies) of a large dataset. Indeed, when more generic characteristics are present, the competitive learning algorithm becomes computationally infeasible.

Competitive Learning

Assume a sequence of statistical samples of a set of observations, $x = x(t) \in \mathbb{R}^n$, where it is the time coordinate and a set of variable reference vectors $\{m_i(t) : m_i \in \mathbb{R}^n, i = 1, 2, 3, ..., k\}$. Assume that $m_i(0)$ has been initialised via random selection. If $x(t)$ can be simultaneously compared with each $m_i(t)$ at each successive time interval, then the best matching $m_i(t)$ is to be updated to match more closely to the current $x(t)$. If the comparison is based on some distance measure $d(x, m_i)$, altering m_i must be such that, if $i = c$ is the index of the best matching reference vector, then $d(x, m_c)$ is decreased and all other reference vectors m_i with $i \neq c$ are left intact. This enables the reference vectors to become specifically attuned to different domains of the input variable x. Again, about the class example above, each student will have an affinity for a particular subject of question asked, becoming subject matter experts when presented with more examples of the same type.

Vector Quantization (VQ) is a method that produces an approximation to a continuous probability density function, $p(x)$, of the vector input variable, x, using a finite number of codebook vectors[3] m_i. Once the codebook is chosen, the approximation of x involves finding the reference vector m_c closest to x. One method of the optimal placement m_i of minimises E, the expected r^{th} power of the reconstruction error. The reconstruction error is given by:

$$E = \int \|x - m_c\|^r p(x) dx \tag{1}$$

Where dx is the volume differential in the x space and the index $c = c(x)$ of the best matching codebook vector is a function of the input vector x. Thus, one needs to minimise the distance between x and m_c:

$$\|x - m_c\| = \min_i \{\|x - m_c\|\} \tag{2}$$

Generally, no closed-form solution for the optimal placement of m_i is possible. Thus, iterative approximation techniques must be used. Equation (2) defines a placement of the codebook vectors into a signal space such that their point density function is an approximation to $p(x)^{\frac{n}{(n+r)}}$ where n is the dimensionality of and x and m_i. In practical applications, n is strictly greater than r ($n \gg r$) (there must necessarily be more observations than dimensions) and the optimal VQ can be shown to approximate $p(x)$. In problems where the above equality does not hold, one can turn to models of artificial intelligence.

---

[3] Each vector is quantised to a code vector. The collection of code vectors is thus the codebook.

AI MODELS

To mimic the thought processes of the human brain, artificial intelligence models can be categorized into expert systems and neural networks. The former uses knowledge-based systems to arrive at a decision while the latter relies on computational techniques to provide as accurate as possible an estimate of the output data.

Expert Systems

An expert system (ES), as defined by Plant and Stone (1991) is a "computer program that mimics the human reasoning process, which relies on logic, belief, rules of thumb, opinion and experience." (Plant & Stone, 1991, p.1241). This reasoning process is coded as "IF-THEN" statements—a logic statement that has several premises, which if satisfied, imply a conclusion. For example, if "today is Monday" (premise 1) and "it is 8 AM" (premise 2) then "I have a meeting" (conclusion). While the ES can mimic humans, it is sensitive to incomplete and noisy data (Fu, 1995). Further, some forms of human reasoning cannot be fully captured by logical "IF-THEN" statements. Fu (1995) shows that an ES works in a sequential manner, whereas an ANN works in parallel. In other words, an ES can only be provided with a single input at a time in contrast to multiple inputs being provided to an ANN. Thus, they can be viewed as complimentary approaches where the ANN will learn from the input data while the ES extracts decisions from the output of the ANN. An ES also differs from an ANN in the manner of information processing, connectivity, self-learning ability, fault tolerance and relation to neurobiology.

NEURAL NETWORKS

Any form of explanatory analysis on share returns makes the implicit assumption that publicly available information has a relationship to future share returns. Such information could range from economic variables, fundamental (accounting-based) variables to rumor and speculation. This assumption clearly violates the EMH that states that it is impossible to forecast future prices as all relevant information is already accounted for in current market prices. When new information enters the market, prices will adjust instantaneously in a random manner according to the random walk hypothesis. This line of reasoning implies that the best forecast of future share prices is the current share price, thus resulting in a random walk model. A major caveat of studies that show the contrary, which is exposed by proponents of the EMH, is that the evidence presented relies on a linear dependence between the share price and the independent variables. Practically, it is reasonable to infer those non-linear relationships do exist between economic and financial variables. Given this inference, one can then proceed to model these relationships. However, this model-driven approach requires that the model first be specified before estimation of the parameters can commence. Neural networks have thus been introduced to model financial problems precisely because of the reason outlined above. They are capable of non-linear modelling without any *a priori* knowledge about the relationship between the input and output variables. Desai and Bharati (1998) test the predictability of four asset class returns using a neural network. If a neural network is mistakenly applied to linear data, the network will either be relatively computationally expensive to train compared to simpler linear models or will overfit the data and learn the noise in the series. Thus, to avoid the latter, one should first investigate the series for neglected non-linearity before attempting to use a neural network to predict any future values. Using two popular tests of the sort, Desai and Bharati (1998) test the return series for large stocks, small stocks, corporate bonds, and government bonds. They find that non-linearities do exist in large stocks and corporate bonds and attempt to fit a neural network to predict future values of these two-asset class returns. The neural network outperformed both a linear regression and GARCH model, showing that over the sample period covered, neural networks are more suitable for modelling non-linear behavior of asset classes.

Notwithstanding their ability to perform non-linear modelling, the accuracy of results from a neural network is heavily biased towards the ability of the researcher. In other words, a neural network is only as successful at predicting future prices based on the inputs received (which are selected by the researcher). Often, no justification is given for the selection criteria of input variables. It is apparent that the inclusion (or exclusion) of (irrelevant) relevant input variables can be detrimental to the success of the network. Given some background on neural networks, one proceeds to be informed of their development since inception.

NEURO-COMPUTING HISTORY

Nelson and Illingworth (1990) provide a primer on neuro-computing history, by dividing it into six phases.

The Conception Era, from 1890 to 1949

The era of conception includes the first development in brain studies and the understanding of how the brain processes information. It is believed that the first work on brain activity was published by the seminal work on psychology by James (1890) as cited in Nelson and Illingworth (1990).

> Psychology is the Science of Mental Life, both of its phenomena and of their conditions. The phenomena are such things as we call feelings, desires, cognitions, reasonings, decisions and the like; and, superficially considered, their variety and complexity are such as to leave a chaotic impression on the observer. The most natural and consequently the earliest way of unifying the material were, first, to classify it as well as might be... This is the orthodox "spiritualistic" theory of scholasticism and of common sense. Another and a less obvious way of unifying the chaos is to seek common elements *in* the diverse mental facts rather than a common agent behind

them, and to explain them constructively by the various forms of arrangement of those elements, as one explains houses by stones and bricks... The very Self or *ego* of the individual comes in this way to be viewed no longer as the pre-existing source of the representations, but rather as their last and most complicated fruit. (James, 1890, pp.1–2, as cited in Nelson & Illingworth, 1990)

Given the above reasoning, scientists began to determine how the brain processes information to arrive at a conclusion, giving birth to the idea of mapping and eventually automating this process. In the field of theoretical neurophysiology, the nervous system is seen as a network of neurons that have some threshold to being excited to generate an impulse. The first published work on neural networks was that of McCulloch and Pitts (1943), where the authors used an ANN to compute arithmetic and logical functions. In one of the authors' previous works, a hypothesis was proposed that the response of any neuron could be equated to a proposition that provided the threshold to be excited. In other words, one can symbolically describe the activity of a neuron in terms of receiving an input, passing a threshold, and resulting in excitation of the neuron itself. It was found that to each reaction of a neuron, there was a corresponding simple proposition, implying that either some other simple proposition, alone or combined with others, led to the neuron being activated. McCulloch and Pitts (1943) provide a form of calculus to the functioning of the neuron by assuming the simplest case of total or zero activation (the neuron has a binary state of either being excited or not). In addition, the authors conclude that if their networks are undefined, so too are the results of the networks. The Conception era ended with the work of Hebb (1949) who provided the first primer on neuro-computing, indeed, in similar spirit to the works of Graham and Dodd (1934). McCulloch and Pitts' (1943) work was later reinforced by Hebb (1949), who stated that neural pathways are strengthened each time they are used, enabling learning to occur in humans.

Gestation and Birth, During the 1950s

After establishing that a biological neuron can be represented, developments to hardware and software marked the time of the gestation era of neuro-computing. The formation of the Dartmouth Artificial Intelligence research project provided the foundations for neuro-computing research (Nelson & Illingworth, 1990). This two-month research project was a brain storming session to transform the calculus of McCulloch and Pitts (1943) into workable computer algorithms.

Early Infancy, During the Late 1950s

With the work of von Neumann (1958) on "The Computer and the Brain," the era of early infancy in neuro-computing began. Rosenblatt (1958) also built the first neurocomputer, the Rosenblatt perceptron, which is considered the oldest ANN hardware. A year later, but published in 1960, Widrow and Hoff (1960) develop a Multiple Adaptive Linear Elements program called *MADALINE*, to recognize binary patterns when reading streaming bits from a phone line and predict the next bit. This was the first neural network applied to a real-world problem and is still in use today.

Stunted Growth, From 1961 to 1981

In later work, Widrow and Hoff (1960) develop a learning algorithm to adjust the weights of a neighboring perceptrons if the perceptron in question has a large error term. While Rosenblatt (1958) published extensive work on neuro-computing, the era of stunted growth was marked by efforts by Minsky and Pappert (1969) to discredit the work on ANNs. The authors argued that there could be no extension from a single layered network to a multi-layered network and that the learning function in use by many researchers was flawed, as it could not be mathematically differentiable across the entire learning function (it did not produce a continuous output). This resulted in much research being devoted to the area of artificial intelligence as opposed to neuro-computing. In other words, researchers began to practically solve for how a network could learn as opposed to the biological and psychological processes behind the learning itself. With the advent of artificial intelligence, some began to question the philosophical concerns over creating machines that could think.

Late Infancy I, From 1982 to 1985

With the few researchers that remained in the field of neuro-computing, the field began to re-emerge during the early 1980s. The most notable introduction during this period is the Hopfield network by Hopfield (1984), designed for image recognition. In a Hopfield network, each neuron has a sigmoid input-output function as this enables a continuous value to be populated in the range [0,1] as opposed to a simple binary value instead. The author shows that this deterministic system is quite like the stochastic model of McCulloch and Pitts (1943).

Late Infancy II, From 1986 to 2000

Similarly, the most notable introduction during the late infancy period is the introduction of the back-propagation algorithm by Werbos (1974). Based on his doctoral thesis, the author defines an algorithm that calculates the mathematical derivatives of a single target quantity in relation to a large set of input quantities. The BP algorithm is now one of the most common learning algorithms for neural networks and has now been extended for use across time series data, including stock returns. Some of this literature is discussed below.

NEURAL NETWORK APPLICATION

Basheer and Hajmeer (2000) categorize seven problems that ANNS can be used to solve. Where relevant, a financial example will be used to describe the problem that can be solved by the ANN.

Pattern Classification

An ANN can be used to classify an output based on several properties that exist in the input data. For example, an ANN can be used to classify whether a share price moves up or down, whether an investor should buy or sell a share, *inter alia*. Garth et al. (1996) state that an ANN does not require the assumption of linearity in the data and as such can be applied to non-linear separable data. Provided with a set of data and set characteristics, the network identifies common characteristics between two observations. The most prominent characteristic is then compared to other data points, resulting in a group of data being formed with similar characteristics that are sufficiently different to other groups.

Clustering

Similar to pattern classification, clustering involves an exploration and classification of the differences and similarities in the input data (in pattern classification, the network is given the patterns to find, whereas in clustering, the network is left to discover whatever patterns may exist in the data). The input data is then assigned to a cluster (or class) based on what the network perceives as similar characteristics. This contrasts with pattern classification, where the patterns are pre-specified. In clustering, the patterns are not specified, and the ANN discovers them. Ungrouped data is grouped by the network examining each data point and identifying unique characteristics to separate the data into groups. This technique can be considered when finding relevant factors to use in an asset-pricing model. Without any *a priori* knowledge, the researcher does not know which of the candidate factors selected will be useful in say, explaining returns.

Modelling

The most typical use of an ANN is to train it to model output data. According to Hecht-Nielsen (1988), multilayer ANNs can be considered to approximate any arbitrary function to any specified degree of accuracy, given the variety of learning algorithms and network architectures available. Modelling is mainly used when no theoretical model is available or to substitute an analytically complex theoretical model. In the former case, one provides empirical evidence stemming from the curiosity of the researcher. This evidence is then presented as a hypothesis and subject to testing. The more tests that are conducted on the hypothesis that favor a particular outcome of the hypothesis (reject or fail to reject), leads the hypothesis to be upgraded to a principle (where an overwhelming majority of the results are in favor of a particular outcome) or ultimately a law (all results are of the same consensus). Quite like a regression line, the network attempts to fit a curve (line) to a set of data points while minimizing the distance between itself and the point. The modelling aspect attempts to explain behavior of the data, and not extrapolate to unknown data points.

Forecasting

Often used in tandem with modelling, an ANN can be used to forecast a time series after the series has been modelled. The network can be used to predict out-of-sample observations of the time series. Once a relationship (curve) has been determined (fitted), the researcher can then extrapolate to this to data out of the sample used in the modelling exercise.

Optimization

For problems that require an objective to be maximized or minimized subject to a set of constraints, an ANN can be used. Pham (1994) found ANNs to be more efficient in solving optimization problems that were complex and non-linear in nature. The classical example of portfolio optimization can be used here. An ANN can be used to find the optimal weights of a portfolio such that the portfolio is mean-variance efficient.

Association

An interesting area of application for ANNs is to reconstruct patterns or data that are missing or incomplete. The ANN is trained on noise-free data and is then used to classify noisy data. This can be used to, for example, reconstruct an image that is only partially visible. In the field of interest rate mathematics, one often needs to interpolate or extrapolate yields based on limited information. While these formulae do exist, an ANN can also be used in this regard.

Control

Lastly, an ANN can be used to monitor a system such that the outputs of the network (used as inputs to the system) follow a predefined set of rules. For example, an ANN can be used to ensure that the results from an ES remain tractable.

Hardin (2002) suggests that neural networks were developed in part due to the ordinal revolution in economics and decision theory. As the choices of economic agents have a social and interactive context, one needs to construct a means of mapping all potential and actual responses from the interaction of these agents. As our choices have social and interactive elements, it becomes near impossible to theoretically describe all potential paths from these responses and interactions. Thus, Hardin (2002) argues that these models exhibit a fundamental indeterminacy. It is impossible to practically describe all possible interactions and responses. Assuming the rational individual understands the product of their interactions with others, it follows that the reactions of those other participants may not necessarily be similar or unique—like the "prisoner's dilemma." When the element of time is added to these models, the agents may react quite differently to what was assumed by the other agents. These time-based models would be dependent upon some initial condition, which would cause a chaotic series of actions to emanate from each change in condition. Further assuming that a complex model can be constructed and empirically tested, the problem of aggregation arises, where information contained in the individual data are lost due to aggregation. This can be observed through application of Arrow's Impossibility Theorem (Arrow, 1950). Aggregation of preferences into a general choice rule makes it impossible to determine the optimal allocation of resources in the face of disagreement.[4]

ANNs assume ambiguity[5] in the ability of the researcher—the researcher does not know that he is incapable of conceiving, designing or constructing a complicated, interactive model of human behavior. Thus, the alternative would be to learn from past observations, without imposing a determinate principle on it (Krippendorf, 2002). In economics and finance, this does not necessarily pose a problem as initial conditions are dependent on future expectations—the price of a stock today does not necessarily depend solely on its previous price, but also on the forces of supply and demand for it. Applying an ANN to an economic or financial problem, the focus would be to detect and test for non-linear relationships, as they are more likely to be present than linear relationships, according to Granger (1991). While neural networks are capable of processing voluminous amounts of data, they lack insightful imagination (Weiss & Kulikowski, 1991). In other words, while they are capable of processing voluminous data and performing calculations beyond the natural ability of humans, the results of ANNs are essentially taken to be true, provided the data and the network itself is adequate.

Advantages and Disadvantages of ANNs

The use of ANNs over conventional statistical methods presents many useful advantages. First, ANNs can analyze complex patterns in the data with a high degree of accuracy. Second, there are no assumptions made as to the underlying distribution of the data. They thus provide an unbiased analysis, especially when the relationships between variables do not fit an assumed model. Maasoumi et al. (1994) stress that since time-series data is dynamic, it is necessary to have non-linear tools to discover any relationships among the data. They conclude that ANNs are the best at discovering such relationships. Given that not all data sets

---

[4] The theorem is most described in an example of an election. Assume a finite set of candidates for the election, a finite set of voters and their individual preferences for outcomes. These preferences are unrestricted - they are independent of other influences. The theorem states that it is not possible to derive a complete and consistent social choice rule exclusively from the individual preferences, except in dictatorships.

[5] Ambiguity is defined as unknown outcomes with an unknown distribution.

are complete, ANNs can perform well with missing or incomplete data. The ANN can readjust its connection weights to account for the new data presented to it, enabling a dynamic updating of the node thresholds, and providing a more accurate forecast. In comparison to an econometric model, it is easier for an ANN to forecast data over short intervals, given that the argument of anomalous characteristics disappearing when data is aggregated. If the ANN is used for solving an economic or financial problem, this advantage is quite appealing. To circumvent data aggregation, data of differing frequencies is thus used in this study to provide robustness.

Given the complex nature of economic and financial systems, it is difficult (if not impossible) to develop a model that accounts for all possible reactions and counter-reactions. If one tries to account for all possible outcomes and dynamic interactions, the resulting model becomes both overly complex and impractical to test. Thus, using principles such as profit or utility maximization produce inaccurate results. Recall that the most important maxim in the AMH is that of survival—not necessarily of profit or utility maximization. ANNs, while not attempting to provide a complete model of the system, attempt to emulate it. ANNs can handle the indeterminacy of the system by utilizing probability and statistics; or by using fuzzy logic on the input and output data. The activation function can thus be adjusted accordingly. While the ANN does not solve the indeterminacy problem, it provides a means of reducing it; thereby allowing forecasts and predictions to be carried out with some degree of accuracy (often higher than traditional econometric methods). This is indirectly tested by using differing frequency data in this study as well comparing the result of the neural network to more traditional econometric models.

As much as an ANN solves many problems, there are also flaws in utilizing them. Firstly, ANN development is often left to the researcher in that there is no structured methodology available for constructing an ANN. Further, the output quality may be unpredictable regardless of the architecture of the network. The researcher may have followed each reasonable heuristic in designing an optimal network, but the output may nonetheless be poor. An ANN is also considered to be a "black box" (a system that cannot be fully described despite it accurately predicting output data). As such, it is impossible to determine the relationship between nodes in the hidden layer without further additions (Li, 1994). One such method that has emerged in the recent literature is the use of a Deterministic Finite State Automaton (DFA). These DFAs produce a symbolic representation of how input data is processed and transformed into output data, however, this method is still in its infancy as of time of writing

ANNs can be thought of as autopoietic systems—they produce their own patterns from a set of inputs that are, in turn, used to operate the future production of outputs which are emulative (provide empirical evidence) instead of theoretical (provide theoretical evidence) (Krippendorf, 2002). In contrast, a regression model is usually built around first principles in statistics and physics. Thus, a regression model provides a higher level of structure and explanatory power compared to an ANN. As such, it is important to understand the different types of ANN architecture to determine if the advantages and disadvantages of each are acceptable to the researcher. ANNs usually have long training times that require the researcher to perform multiple iterations to enhance confidence in the predictive ability of the network. Another disadvantage is that neural networks are data dependent. The success of the ANN depends on the input data. In solving financial problems, it is crucial to test the ANN on out-of-sample data as the input data may be inherently different (similar) to the out-of-sample data.

Kanas (2001) developed an ANN for the Dow Jones and Financial Times indices. Tests from both the ANN and a linear model revealed little in predicting directional changes in the indices, however, the non-linearity in share prices was confirmed. An ANN may easily over-fit or under-fit the data, an implication from an indeterminate system. Therefore, an ANN does not contain explicit causal relationships nor is built on first principles.

It should be noted that many of the disadvantages highlighted above can be solved using pre-processed data (for example, using returns instead of raw price levels). As per Schwartz (1995), using a few well-chosen variables will result in a better result than using every known economic variable as inputs. Often, the ES can be used to eliminate either insignificant or highly correlated variables—speeding up the training time and enhancing accuracy. This also adds an element of indeterminacy—the choice of the ES differs each time based on the iteration and choice of expert. More such applications are now discussed, with reference to the use of neural networks as opposed to other AI techniques.

APPLICATION OF ANNS TO FINANCE

Swales and Yoon (1992) test whether an ANN is better at forecasting than multiple discriminant analysis. Given the popularity of the former technique, the limitations of the technique suggest that a non-linear approach may better assist analysts and investors in making investment decisions. The authors show that an ANN is superior at predicting share prices compared to the discriminant analysis method, based on analyzing information content in news alerts from select Fortune 500 companies.

In the insurance arena, Brockett et al. (1994) construct an early warning system to predict insolvency on insured clients. The authors use a feed-forward neural network with the back-propagation learning algorithm and compare its performance against the more traditional measures in the field to predict insolvency, namely discriminant analysis and publicly reported insurance regulator ratings. They find that the neural network shows a high level of predictability and generalization for predicting insolvency two years after the end of their sample period. While it is now known that a feedforward network is not the best architecture to use for time series data, the results of the authors show the power of artificial intelligence techniques in solving relevant issues in finance (or at least in insurance).

In the pricing of derivatives, the most common practice is to use the Black-Scholes option-pricing framework. However, this approach rests on the parametric specification of the dynamics of the underlying asset's price. If there is a misspecification in this stochastic return generating process, then it follows that the price derived from the framework will be error prone. In effect, the success of establishing a true price of the derivative rests on correctly specifying the stochastic process of the underlying asset price. Hutchinson et al. (1994) propose a non-parametric approach for pricing derivatives. By selecting those factors believed to influence the derivative's price, the authors compare the error terms from three different models, a radial basis function network, a multilayer perceptron and a projection pursuit regression (PPR) (a technique unrelated to artificial intelligence, PPR is a means of analyzing high dimensional datasets by examining their lower dimension projections). While the authors do report that the networks are better than other methods, they are hesitant to generalize their findings given the short data period (three years) and single derivative instrument used.

While the ANN is better at prediction, it does not imply that the ANN is a determinate system. Some authors, such as Hill et al. (1994) find that the ANN is comparable to traditional statistical methods. Indeed, the ANN performs as well as the classical regression model at forecasting yearly prices, but better in forecasting monthly and quarterly prices. When non-linearity is present in the data, the ANN can necessarily outperform regressions in modelling human behavior. Kuo and Reitsch (1995) test regression and ANN methods at forecasting data. They use two datasets, one with a dependent variable and a number of explanatory variables (a cross sectional dataset) and the other with a single dependent variable measured across time (a time series dataset). Further employing exponential smoothing techniques to the time series data, the authors find the neural network models generated the most accurate forecasts in both datasets.

Kuan and Liu (1995) investigate the out-of-sample forecasting ability of neural networks in predicting exchange rates. As foreign exchange rates are integrated of order one and their changes are uncorrelated over time, these changes are not linearly predictable. Thus, one needs to employ non-linear methods to forecast them. Utilizing a two-step procedure to estimate and select the appropriate feed-forward and recurrent network, the results from their study are mixed. Out of six daily exchange rates studied (the U.S Dollar, British Pound, Canadian Dollar, Deutsche Mark, Japanese Yen and Swiss Franc) over 1980 to 1985, only two networks offer either significant market timing ability (predicting the correct direction of the future exchange rate) or a lower out of sample error. While their results are not overall in favor of using neural networks to forecast exchange rates, the authors do propose an easily implemented procedure in selecting the best network for use in the modelling exercise. The procedure allows for a family of networks to be estimated that produce the best predictive ability. Thereafter, statistically better estimates for these networks are derived using non-linear least squares regressions. The authors test this procedure and find that it performs well in determining the optimal ANN.

Shachmurove and Witkowska (2001) investigate the dynamic relationships between major world stock markets using neural networks. Using daily data from seven major indices (six country indices and one world index), the authors propose that the daily return on a particular index is a function (contemporaneous and lagged) of other indices. They first apply ordinary least squares regression methods to determine which variables are significant to be input to the neural network, a multilayer perceptron. They find that the neural network predicts daily stock returns better than the more traditional methods of ordinary least squares and general linear regression models. Further, there are different network architectures that exist for each index. The results of their study point towards a simple, yet powerful application of neural networks in predicting stock returns. In the case of the authors, their objective was to determine if there exist interrelations between global stock indices and to determine if a non-parametric model provided superior forecasting ability. Indeed, asset managers and investment banks such as Goldman Sachs and J.P. Morgan utilize ANNs (Shachmurove & Witkowska, 2001). The authors describe how a unit trust by Fidelity Investments bases its portfolio allocation on the recommendations of its ANN. The increased usage of ANNs in business indicates the usefulness of the ANN in solving financial problems and can be considered a pioneering field in the realm of empirical finance.

CASE STUDY

Setting Boundaries for Neural Networks

According to a popular internet meme, there are two types of people in this world: those who can extrapolate from incomplete data. Neural networks will probably struggle with that one.

As quants race to deploy neural networks in finance, they are running into a common problem. Neural networks require huge datasets to train, but they do not always extrapolate well when faced with new situations.

"Neural networks can fit the data very well within the region of training but can produce completely unpredictable and uncontrolled results outside of that," says Michael Konikov, head of quantitative development at Numerix.

Konikov, along with Alexandre Antonov, chief analyst at Danske Bank, and Vladimir Piterbarg, head of quantitative analytics and development at NatWest Markets, propose a two-step solution to this extrapolation problem.

The authors tackle the common issue of approximating a derivatives pricing function using neural networks. They start by approximating the pricing function with a cubic spline, a set of third-degree polynomial curves joined. This allowed them to closely replicate the asymptotes of the pricing function and capture the limits of the function for large values of its parameters.

Asymptotes are normally known or relatively easy to calculate for many common functions in finance, making it possible for the pricing function to be approximated by a spline-like function. By subtracting the cubic spline from the pricing function, they created a function that tends to zero for large values of parameters, de facto eliminating explosive, or uncontrollable values. This effectively reduces the problem to the approximation of a neural network to a pricing function with null asymptotes. Next, an additional mapping function is inserted into the neural network to ensure that, outside a selected domain, asymptotes are kept to zero.

"We look at the expected behavior of the model for large values of input parameters, outside the region where we would normally use neural networks, and incorporate that into the overall approximation," explains Piterbarg.

The paper describes how the technique works on the SABR model, which has the advantage of being neither too simple nor too complex, and for that reason is commonly used to test neural network applications.

"We use the SABR model [to show] the power of our method. The good thing about it is one can calculate its true values for any set of input parameters exactly," Piterbarg says. We look at the expected behavior of the model for large values of input parameters, outside the region where we would normally use neural networks, and incorporate that into the overall approximation Vladimir Piterbarg, NatWest Markets.

The technique, however, is fully general and can be applied to any function that can be approximated with a neural network and has known asymptotes in some dimensions. Piterbarg sees XVA calculation as one possible application.

"It is particularly suitable for complex pricing functions that involve expensive Monte Carlo simulations, like those of Bermudan options or other exotics, with a reasonable number of parameters, like rates, vols etc.," says Antonov. He is planning to "implement it to a low/mid-dimensional problem of a spread option between two SABR rates." Numerix also intends to put the research to work.

"While this technique has not been implemented in our production library yet, we plan to do this at some point in the future," reveals Konikov. Piterbarg himself has been critical of hasty applications of neural networks in finance, comparing them to a hammer looking for a nail. Using classical functional analysis to control extrapolation by neural networks will mitigate some of the risks inherent in deploying this new technology.

"What we're trying to do is focus neural network research in the direction where it actually works together with traditional research," he says.

https://www.risk.net/our-take/7733011/setting-boundaries-for-neural-networks

QUESTIONS

1. Provide examples of the different uses of ANNs in financial services.

2. Discuss circumstances where an ANN is not as effective as more traditional methods.
3. How has the introduction of ANNs changed the face of capital markets?
4. Are ANNs able to effectively replace the role of human beings in financial services?

CHAPTER 6

A FRAMEWORK FOR ARTIFICIAL INTELLIGENCE

Given a problem to solve, Rumelhart et al. (1986) provide a taxonomy for determining the appropriate modelling process. As can be seen from Figure 6.1, the

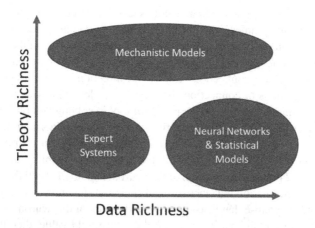

FIGURE 6.1.   Suitability of a Modelling Technique Relative to Data and Theory (adapted from Rumelhart et al., 1986)

A Primer on Business Analytics: Perspectives from the Financial Services Industry, pages 81–101.
81

decision rests on the availability of theory describing the problem at hand, and the data available. Data richness with scarce theory point towards an ANN, whereas both data and theory scarcity point to an ES. Conversely, for problems rich in data and theory, a mechanistic model can be used. Naturally, there will be overlapping areas that are more realistic. For partially understood phenomena (with moderately available data and theory), a semi-empirical model that utilizes all three areas can be used. From the arguments presented, it can be concluded that the realm of finance is rich in data and modestly rich in theory (where, in the strictest sense of the word, finance primarily has a collection of hypotheses which are not independent of the object being explained). Therefore, neural networks and statistical models are most suited to empirically test problems in finance. As most readers are familiar with statistical models, this chapter is devoted to outlining the theoretical components of neural networks.

LEARNING OBJECTIVES

After reading this chapter you should be able to:

- Understand the construction of neural networks from a biological perspective
- Understand a few of the various neural networks that can be used to solve financial problems

A CONCEPTUAL VIEW OF A NEURAL NETWORK

A network consists of nodes and connections where the nodes represent computational units. Input variables would be passed to an input node, processed, and then passed on as an output. The output can either be the final output of the network or further passed on to another input node. Connections allow information to flow between nodes. These connections can be uni-directional or bi-directional. The various combinations of connections between nodes lead to a wide array of outputs, thus making neural networks a powerful tool in solving complex problems.

If one views the nodes as representative of the human brain's neurons, then the network is referred to as an artificial neural network (ANN). The terminology and philosophy of the ANN was inspired by the processing capability of the human brain. Figure 6.2 presents a rendition of the neuron, a biological cell that processes and transmits information via electrical and chemical signaling. These signals are received via the synapse that is located on the dendrite of the neuron. If the signal is sufficiently strong and surpasses a particular threshold value, then the neuron is activated, and a signal is sent through the axon to another synapse. In turn, the latter synapse may be activated, thus *exciting* other neurons. This process is continued until a particular outcome is achieved.

The understanding outlined above provides an abstraction of the workings of an ANN. An ANN will consist of inputs (synapses) that map to a particular func-

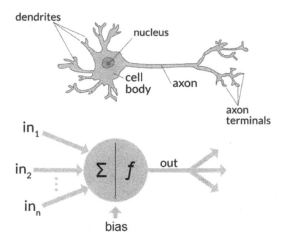

FIGURE 6.2.   Biological Representation of a Neuron (Source: https://towardsda-tascience.com/the-differences-between-artificial-and-biological-neural-networks-a8b46db828b7)

tion (a threshold gate) that determines if the node is activated. Each input is as-signed a weighting that represents the strength of the input. If the strength of the input is sufficiently strong, it passes the threshold and activates the node. The activated node then outputs a variable that serves as either a result or as input to other nodes. This is depicted diagrammatically in Figure 6.2, where an input x_i and corresponding weight w_i is assessed at the linear threshold gate. Those inputs that have a high strength can pass through the gate and result in an output y.

The weights applied to each signal can either be positive or negative (in which the latter would inhibit activation). A higher weight (in absolute terms) would lead to a stronger signal. The weights of the neuron can be adjusted to achieve the desired output. However, when the number of inputs or the number of neurons (or both) is large, the computational complexity of optimizing the weights becomes prevalent. As such, algorithms have been developed to make this task easier. Such algorithms are said to train the network (or alternatively, the network can learn). While many algorithms exist, they can be classified according to their learning strategy. For example, learning by trial and error or learning by back-propagation.

Thus, by changing either the: activation function within the nodes, acceptable threshold value to achieve activation, topology of the network (the flow of infor-mation between nodes), learning algorithms of the network or any combination thereof, a variety of ANNs can be developed. An ANN is effectively a combina-tion of artificial neurons. This primary component is now discussed, followed by a discussion of the perceptron, a group of artificial neurons.

THE ARTIFICIAL NEURON

Rosenblatt (1958) developed the mechanics of the artificial neuron and subsequently, the perceptron. Consider Equation 6.1:

$$y = f(\xi) = \begin{cases} 1, if \sum_{i=1}^{n} w_i x_i \succeq b \\ \\ 0, if \sum_{i=1}^{n} w_i x_i \prec b \end{cases} \tag{6.1}$$

A set of i inputs, ξ, are fed into a (linear) function, f. If the inner (dot) product of each input with corresponding weight, w_i, is sufficient to activate the neuron, then the output, y, takes on a binary value of unity. The threshold value that determines activation is referred to as the bias of the neuron, b. Weights that are positive are said to enhance the signal and excite the neuron, whereas weights that are negative are said to inhibit the signal.

THE PERCEPTRON

In relation to Equation 6.1 above, there is a linear threshold gate that needs to be passed by the signal to activate the neuron. This network architecture is referred as a single layer perceptron. One would train the perceptron by calibrating the weights based on the error between the actual and desired output. The error term is a function of all the weights in the perceptron and forms an irregular multidimensional complex hyperplane (an *n-dimensional* space, with planes that are not of equal size and contain complex numbers). Specialized searching techniques would be employed to find the global minima of this hyperplane, resulting in the optimal network, as the global minima corresponds to the smallest error term (and therefore a more accurate fit of the data). By this definition, it can be inferred that the global minima of the error hyperplane do not necessarily imply that the error term is eliminated in its entirety. Indeed, the global minima can be considered the acceptable standard based on the judgement of the network architect, like how a researcher would judge the Root Mean Squared Error (RMSE) of a regression to be acceptable. Secondly, the single layer perceptron is only suitable for linearly separable problems. In such problems, two classes can easily be distinguished on either side of the hyperplane, depicted in Figure 6.3. For those problems that are non-linearly separable, a multilayer perceptron is used. If there were numerous thresholds to surpass, then the perceptron is referred as multi-layered. In such an architecture, further layers of nodes are placed between the input and output layer. These are referred to as hidden layers, and consequently the nodes within them are "hidden." More sophisticated learning algorithms were developed to train the network in reducing the error term to an acceptable level. These algorithms, along with the type of network used, create a hierarchy of neural networks where one can select the best network architecture based on the problem at hand.

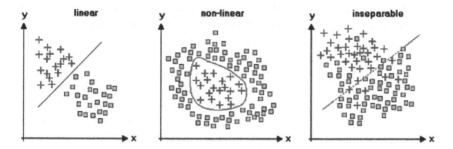

FIGURE 6.3.   Types of Problems That Can Be Solved by a Network (Source: http://www.statistics4u.com/fundstat_eng/cc_data_structure.html)

NEURAL NETWORK HIERARCHY

Angus (1991) provides guidelines on selecting the best network for the application at hand. The author suggests that the type of network be guided on its applicability to the problem. Roughly, the problem statement can be split between time-variant and time-invariant problems. A time-variant problem would relate to some spatio-temporal pattern, where the time stamp of the variable(s) in question plays some role in the output. In contrast, a time-invariant problem does not require any dependence on a time stamp.

Generally, feed-forward networks are sufficient for learning time-invariant problems, however, there are networks, such as Tapped Delay Neural Networks (TDNNs) that can be used. Angus (1991) argues that the use of hidden states in a neural network (NN) expands the range of applications for the NN. Recurrent Neural Networks (RNNs) can be used to model time-varying problems, recognize patterns or for forecasting purposes. These networks can model non-linear chaotic, dynamic systems and in principle, should be able to predict future values of the output variable. As such, the family of RNNs is considered more applicable to the problem of modelling cyclical market efficiency. A non-linear autoregressive with exogenous inputs (NARX) RNN will be used and is described in detail later. The ensuing sub-sections describe types of neural networks, with each subsequent network considered an enhancement of the prior network discussed.

Feed-Forward Neural Networks (FFNN)

A FFNN can learn to map inputs to outputs. It has a static structure that can be used to detect spatial patterns in data—data that is independent of time. In a feed-forward neural network, input variables from each training sample are used simultaneously. The weighted output of these units (computed from the first processing layer) is then entered again simultaneously into the second processing layer (a hidden layer). This process continues until the weighted output of the units reaches the final output layer. The output layer then issues a prediction for a given set of samples. A popular training algorithm used in this type of model is the back-propagation algorithm. Briefly, this algorithm assigns a "responsibility" to each processing unit in the network for mismatches. This "responsibility" is achieved through assigning a gradient (threshold) to the activation function, where mismatches are then sent back to the previous (hidden) layer. This previous layer then modifies the weights of the input data set to minimize the error from the final network output. The back-propagation algorithm is a supervised learning procedure that attempts to minimize the error between the desired and predicted outputs. The output value for a given unit can be represented by:

$$O_j = G\left(\sum_{i=1}^{n} w_{i,j} x_i - \theta_j\right) \tag{6.2}$$

where x_i is the output value of the ith unit in the preceding layer, W_{ij} is the weight on the connection from the ith unit, θ_j is the threshold, n is the number of units in the preceding layer, and G is the activation function.

Graphically, a feed-forward neural network can be seen in Figure 6.4. There are n input data samples, fed into n input layers. These outputs are then passed onto a number of hidden layers for further processing. The output from the hidden layers is then passed onto the final output layers, resulting in K classes of samples. Vellido et al. (1999) claim that feed-forward neural networks are well suited to applications within banking (such as customer segmentation or credit scoring) as they can correctly classify and predict the dependent variable. These applications rely on a cross-sectional dataset of banking information, as opposed to a time series dataset.

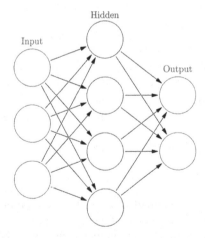

FIGURE 6.4. A Feed-forward neural network (Source: https://automaticaddison.com/artificial-feedforward-neural-network-with-backpropagation-from-scratch/)

A common pitfall with these models lies in under-fitting (there are too few neurons) or over-fitting (there are too many neurons). Peterson et al. (1995) suggest using an *n-fold* cross-validation approach. The data sample is randomly partitioned into *n* equal sized folds and the network is trained *n* times. In each training simulation, one-fold is omitted from the data and the resultant output of the network is compared to this omitted fold (the validation set). An alternative technique, known as 'early stopping,' is suggested by Demuth and Beale (1998). The researcher can stop the network once overfitting is observed and compare the results at this early stopping phase to the validation set.

Probabilistic Neural Networks (PNN)

The Probabilistic neural network is used mainly for pattern classifications. It is a parallel implementation of Parzen windows (a classification technique for estimating non-parametric density functions) and is based on the estimated probability density function for various classes. The network learns instantaneously from the sample data, defines a probability density function, and computes the non-linear decision boundaries between classes—like the Bayes optimal criterion.

The density function can be represented as:

$$f_1(x) = \frac{1}{(2\pi)^{0.5p} \sigma^p n} \sum_{i=1}^{n} z_i \qquad (6.3)$$

where $f_1(x)$ is the probability density function estimator for class 1, p is the dimensionality of training vector, $z_i = e^{\left[\frac{-D_i}{2\sigma^2}\right]}$ is the output of hidden neuron, $D_i = (x - u_i)^T (x - u_i)$, is the distance between the input vector x and the training vector **u** from category 1, and σ is a smoothing parameter.

Figure 6.5 shows the architecture of a PNN. For a given set of inputs, Hidden Layer 1 in the figure computes the distances from the input vector to the training vector. This resulting vector indicates how close the input vector is to the output vector. Hidden Layer 2 then adds these elements for each class of inputs to produce a vector of probabilities as its output. The output layer then picks the maximum of these probabilities and places it into specific output classes.

Time Delay Neural Networks (TDNN)

TDNNs are a form of feed-forward neural networks that have tapped input delays, as shown in Figure 6.6. Principally, a Time-Delay Neural Network is an extended MLP (multilayer perceptron). TDNNs apply time delays on connections, which allow the neural network to have a "memory," to deal with various time-series forecasts. This type of NN specifically addresses the time series dependence of data on preceding values. A TDNN can allow inputs to arrive at hidden units

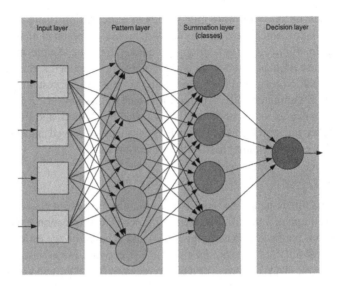

FIGURE 6.5. A Probabilistic Neural Network (Source: https://developer.ibm.com/tutorials/ba-intro-data-science-2/)

at different points in time, thus allowing the various inputs to be stored for a long enough period to have a significant influence on subsequent inputs. The output pattern at a specific point in time is a function of the inputs for that time, as well as the inputs for a prior number of time periods. TDNNs are said to function like a moving average regression model or a finite impulse response filter.

Effectively, by the formulation of T time delays, Δt, every neuron has access to each input value at $T+1$ different point in time. The neurons in the neural network can therefore identify relationships between current and previous input values. Furthermore, the network can estimate functions that take prior input signals into account[1] (Kaiser, 1994). The input vector, $\mathbf{X}$, consists of past samples that are $n*p$ periods in the past

$$\mathbf{X} = \left[x_{t-p}, x_{t-2p}, \ldots, x_{t-np} \right]^{T} \tag{6.4}$$

TDNNs can be used for non-linear prediction of a stationary time series. It uses the error back-propagation algorithm for learning. This method uses gradient descent to find the global minimum of the mean squared error term. Kaiser (1994) posits that traditional methods that are used to speed up back-propagation learning can also be applied to the TDNN. Furthermore, the author states that delayed or scaled input signals can be dealt with by utilizing the original definition of the

---

[1] Such functions may depend on the derivative of the input.

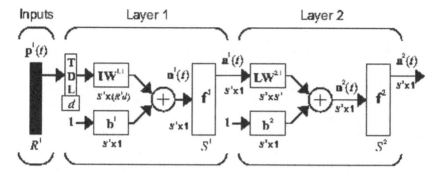

FIGURE 6.6. A Time Delay Neural Network (Source: https://www.mathworks.com/help/deeplearning/ug/design-time-series-time-delay-neural-networks.html)

TDNN, which requires all links of a neuron that are coupled to one input to be identical.[2] However, TDNNs are difficult to implement due to the large number of input nodes.

Non-Linear Autoregressive Models with Exogenous Inputs (NARX)

NARX recurrent neural networks are a form of non-linear models that determine current output values from past input and past output values. A NARX network can be described as follows:

$$y(t) = f\left(u(t-D_u),\ldots,u(t-1),u(t),y(t-D_y),\ldots,y(t-1)\right) \quad (6.5)$$

where $u(t)$ and $y(t)$ represent the input and output respectively of the network, D_u and D_y are the lags of the input and output respectively; and f is a non-linear function.

NARX NNs train and converge much faster compared to their traditional NN counterparts. They are also quite adept at learning long-term dependencies (Lin, et al., 1996) and can store information over extended periods of time.

ISSUES IN ANN DEVELOPMENT

The success or failure of a network at its task is often heavily weighted towards the ability of the researcher to circumvent certain issues in data collection, processing, and network training. This section discusses the most pertinent of these issues and their influence on the result of the network in matching its output to the actual data.

---

[2] For control purposes, current and past inputs may be assigned individual weights (Kaiser, 1994).

Database Size and Partitioning

Perhaps the most detrimental issue to using an ANN in research, the sample size needs to adequate enough for training and testing, without being too large to affect the accuracy of the ANN. Conceptually, the sample size should be large enough to account for possible known variations in the definition of the problem to be solved. An example would be to use a training sub-sample that covers a market cycle. The sample is partitioned into a training, testing and validation sub-sample. The training sample should be described as above—sufficiently large to cover possible known variations in the data. The testing sub-sample should be sufficiently different to that in the training sub-sample, without being considered completely unrelated. An example would be to use a testing sub-sample that covers a market cycle that is different to the one used in training. Lastly, the validation sub-sample is used after the optimal neural network is modelled. Once again, it must be sufficiently different from the previous data, within reason. An example would again be to use data that covers a market cycle, different from the previous sub-samples.

No formal methods exist for determining the optimal sample sizes besides heuristics. Given the diverse possibilities that may exist in a dataset, one needs to use some heuristic that ensures a balance between data for training, testing and validation. For example, Baum and Haussler (1989) propose that the minimum sample size for the training sub-sample be equal to the product of the number of connection weights and the inverse of the minimum acceptable error—similar to traditional regression techniques, one should ensure that there are more observations than there are variables used in the regression. Haykin (1994) suggests an example-to-weight ratio of 0.10, while Masters (1994) suggests a value of 0.4. An alternative approach is to partition the sample using relative percentages. Looney (1996) suggests that 65% be used for training, 25% for testing and 10% for validation.

Data Pre-Processing, Balancing and Enrichment

To accelerate training of the network, the data often needs to be pre-processed. This can be achieved by removing noise, reducing the number of variables, deletion of outliers and transforming the data (Swingler, 1996). Balancing data becomes important in classification problems. It is a process that aims to evenly (or as close to even as possible) distribute the data between the various classes to prevent bias towards a particular class. Either the over-weighted class can be removed or more examples that represent the under-weighted class can be added. Swingler (1996) suggests using Information Theory to measure the degree of balance in the training sub-sample. The data can be enriched by either providing more observations or adding noisy data that can generate new data. The latter is particularly appealing as it not only adds to the size of the sample, but also tests the accuracy of the network. However, one should not provide an abundance of noisy data less the network learns and extrapolate patterns that do not truly exist. An alternative method, suggested by Hecht-Nielsen (1988), *inter alia*, is to leave out k examples from the training sub-sample and repeat the training phase m times leaving out a different set of k examples each time.

Data Normalization

Normalization or scaling of the data within a uniform range prevents larger numbers from overriding smaller ones and premature saturation of the hidden nodes (Basheer & Hajmeer, 2000). While there is no standard method for normalizing data, an example of doing so would be to scale the data in the range $[\lambda_1, \lambda_2]$ by:

$$x_i = \lambda_1 + (\lambda_2 - \lambda_1) * \left(\frac{z_i - z_i^{min}}{z_i^{max} - z_i^{min}} \right) \tag{6.6}$$

Where x_i is the normalised value of z_i, z_i^{min} and z_i^{max} represent maximum and minimum values of z_i. Masters (1994) suggest that the data be normalised to values near 0 and 1 as opposed to at 0 and 1 to avoid saturation of the sigmoid activation function. If this saturation were to occur, the network will inadvertently activate (inhibit) connections between neurons for no justifiable reason. This would cause the output from the network to have a greater degree of error. Masters (1994) also shows that more complicated techniques may not produce better solutions than that obtained using the above equation. Further, for extremely large values, the logarithm of the data may be used prior to normalization. This would avoid outliers in the data and assist in network training time.

Input and Output Representation

Data representation is an important and critical factor in the design of an ANN according to Masters (1994). It may be possible to convert continuous input data to a discrete, binary form to extract rules from a trained network (Fu, 1995). Other specialized algorithms exist for conversion of continuous variables to discrete form based on the distributions (Kerber, 1992). These algorithms allow flexibility in the use of networks as they are capable of handling both discrete and continuous data, transforming the input or output to enhance network accuracy while still providing a tractable means of examining non-linear processes.

Network Weight Initialization

Initializing network weights involves assigning an initial, zero-mean random number to each connection (Rumelhart *et al.*, 1986). The literature does not agree on the importance of selecting the "correct" initial weight. Li et al. (1993, March) show that selecting the "correct" initial weight can have an effect on network convergence in that the initial weight vector may be stationed on the flat region of the error surface—making convergence a slow process. Others, such as Fahlman

(1988) show that initialization has an insignificant effect on both the convergence and network architecture. Arguably, while a particular initial weight will assist in speeding up the training time, it can be considered unnecessary if the computer hardware available is sophisticated enough to not be affected by the non-initialized weights.

ASCE (2000) suggests that weights be initially assigned to small random values between –0.30 and 0.30. Alternatively, weights can be assigned values uniformly sampled from the range $\left[\dfrac{-r}{N_j}, \dfrac{r}{N_j}\right]$ where r is a real number and N_j is the number of connections feeding into neuron j (Haykin, 1994). By providing a range of values, one can narrow down the parameter search for the neural network, making it train faster (notwithstanding the previous statement on the capabilities of the computer hardware used).

The Back-Propagation Learning Rate, η

Apart from data processing and narrowing the search parameter for neuron weights, one can adjust the parameters of the learning algorithm. While a large value for the learning rate will accelerate training, the search algorithm on the error surface may never converge—leading to over-fitting of the model. However, a small value for the learning rate may result in the network taking too much time to converge on a solution. Authors (Wythoff, 1993; Zupan & Gasteiger, 1991; and Fu, 1995) have suggested learning rates between 0.1 and 1.0; 0.3 and 0.6; and 0.0 to 1.0, respectively. Alternatively, an adaptive learning rate may be used which will vary along the course of training. This alternative is appealing as, generally, the distance from a minimum cannot be predicted (one will only know the distance from the minimum after it has been reached). Further, when the search algorithm is far away from the minimum, a larger learning rate is required; whereas a smaller learning rate is required when the search algorithm is near the minimum.

The Back-Propagation Momentum Coefficient, μ

Haykin (1994) states that the inclusion of a momentum term assists in stabilizing the search algorithm for the global minimum. A higher momentum coefficient will accelerate the weight updates and reduce the risk of the search algorithm not converging. However, it also increases the risk of over-fitting. Like the learning rate, either a constant or adaptive value can be used. Wythoff (1993) suggests a learning rate between 0.4 and 0.9 whereas Fu (1995) suggests a rate between 0.0 and 1.0. Others, such as Zupan and Gasteiger (1991) suggest a combined learning rate and momentum coefficient approximately equal to unity. An adaptive momentum coefficient will fluctuate as the training progresses. This technique can be used in conjunction with the methods suggested above, in that as the momentum coefficient increases, the learning rate decreases. Practically, the value of the momentum coefficient also impacts the computer storage space of the researcher.

The Activation Function, σ

A correctly specified activation function is important in the development of an ANN. The choice of activation function is dependent on the objective of the ANN. For example, step functions can be used to indicate whether a neuron is simply activated or not, regardless of the magnitude of activation. ANNs that use back-propagation algorithms usually use a sigmoid function as it has properties of both continuity and differentiability on the real number line. While the advantages of using a particular function over another is not yet understood according to Hassoun (1995), Moody and Yarvin (1992) show that the choice of activation function does affect the success of the ANN. Indeed, if the activation function leads to a saturation of values at its bounds, neurons may be inappropriately activated (inhibited) leading to a larger error term.

Convergence Criteria

An ANN may be said to converge if: 1) the training error is acceptable () or 2) the gradient error is acceptable or 3) there is cross-validation of the output. Basheer and Hajmeer (2000) state that the last criterion is more reliable, at the cost of computing time, power, and abundance of data. Thus, many researchers use the first or second criteria, or a derivation thereof. For example, one can use the coefficient of determination, R^2, or the standard square error, SSE[3], given by:

$$SSE = \frac{1}{N}\sum_{p=1}^{N}\sum_{i=1}^{M}\left(t_{p,i} - O_{p,i}\right)^2 \qquad (6.7)$$

Where $O_{p,i}$ and $t_{p,i}$ are the actual and target solution of the ith output node on the pth training example of N examples and M output nodes. Such an approach incorporates a measure of complexity in the network architecture and was introduced by Garth *et al.* (1996). A plot of the SSE leads to Figure 6.7. As can be seen, there is an initial drop in the SSE followed by a flattening of the training curve. The former is due to the learning success of the network, while the latter is due to either over-fitting (many hidden nodes) or to over-learning (a large number of training cycles). The optimal network is defined as that which minimizes the SSE and either the number of hidden nodes or the number of training cycles. Lakshmanan (1997) suggests that the convergence criterion for classification problems should be based on the percentage of examples classified (In)correctly rather than relying on the absolute deviation from the target output.

---

[3] Alternate measures, such as the Mean Squared Error (MSE), Root MSE, or Mean Absolute Percentage Error (MAPE), can be used. The first two measures are scale dependent and have the advantage of being the most common and statistically relevant. The latter is scale independent and has the advantage of not being sensitive to outliers (Hyndman and Koehler, 2006).

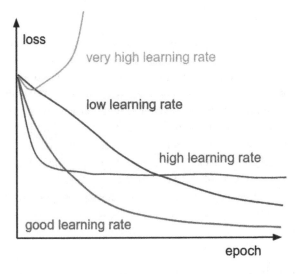

FIGURE 6.7. Depiction of finding the optimal neural network (Source: https://www.kdnuggets.com/2019/11/designing-neural-networks.html)

Number of Training Cycles

The most intuitive (and perhaps best) approach to determine the optimal number of training cycles is through trial and error. While many training cycles may be beneficial in assisting learning, it may lead to over-training of the network and a complete recall of the data (as opposed to a prediction). While the SSE of the network may not follow a strictly smooth path, one can consider a significant increase in SSE (assuming a decreasing SSE) to indicate that the optimum network configuration has been reached.

Modes of Training

Training an ANN can be achieved through either example-by-example or batch training or both (Zupan & Gasteiger, 1991). In the former, each example is presented to the network independently. Once the first example has been learnt (the SSE is acceptable), the second example is then fed to the network. This process then continues. While this method may be computationally simpler, it relies on the integrity of the data—if the initial example was poor, the initial (optimal) weights could falsely lead the network in predicting other examples with little or no accuracy. Batch training, in contrast, updates the connection weights once all examples have been fed to the network. The optimal network is determined by the minimum average error across all examples in the batch. The next batch is presented to the network and is processed using the weights from the previous iteration. Batch training presents an appealing alternative as it represents the connection weights with more accuracy (due to the averaging of the SSE), however the network is more likely to be trapped in a local minimum, leading to a larger error term when a lower one is possible. Further, more computation power and storage are required (Zupan & Gasteiger, 1991). Randomizing the order of the batches has been offered as a solution to the local minimum problem as the network is trained on "more" data to verify patterns it has detected. However, randomizing data is limited to time invariant data—in a time series dataset, each observation must remain ordered in time to avoid spurious results.

Size of the Hidden Layer

The optimal number of hidden layers and subsequent hidden nodes is a critical component in network architecture. While the researcher often starts with no *a priori* knowledge on the number of hidden nodes, Basheer (1998) suggests that one hidden layer is sufficient to approximate continuous functions, whereas Masters (1994) suggests two hidden layers for discontinuous functions. A network with too few hidden layers cannot differentiate between complex patterns whereas too many hidden layers lead to generalization of untrained data If too many hidden nodes are used, the non-linear curve is of a much higher order than considered feasible. If too few hidden nodes are used, one usually finds a linear relationship between the dependent and independent variables, when diagnostic tests reveal the existence of a non-linear relationship.

The optimal number of hidden layers can be thus considered a function of input and output vector sizes, the size of the data subsets and the degree of non-linearity that may be present in the data. Jadid and Fairbairn (1996) propose the upper bound on the number of hidden nodes (NHN) be determined as:

$$NHN \approx \frac{N_{Trn}}{R + \left(N_{Inp} + N_{Out}\right)} \tag{6.8}$$

Where N_{Trn} is the number of training patterns from the data, R is a number from 5 to 10 and N_{inp} and N_{Out} represent the number of nodes in the input and output layers respectively. Various other heuristics exist and unfortunately, for those data sets with non-linearity and hysteresis (a time-based dependence of the system's output on current and past inputs), most heuristics may not yield meaningful results (Basheer, 1998). Basheer and Hajmeer (2000) propose that the researcher begin the process using a heuristic and iteratively determine the optimal NHN using either the heuristic or the information obtained from the SSE.

In summary, training a network rests on optimizing the parameters of the network. Table 6.1 presents a concise view of the effect on each parameter if it incorrectly specified (not all of which is a hindrance to the researcher).

TABLE 6.1. Summary of network parameters

Parameter	Parameter Is Too Large (high)	Parameter Is Too Small (low)
NHN	Over-fitting	Under-fitting
Learning rate, η	Unstable connection weights	Slow training speed
Momentum coefficient, μ	Increased risk of over-shooting minimum error	Entrapment in local error minima.
Number of training cycles	Poor generalization of untrained data	Incapable of generalizing data
Size of training subset	Good generalization ability	Poor generalization
Size of testing subset	Can confirm good generalization ability.	Confirmation of poor generalization

LEARNING ALGORITHMS

The ability to learn distinguishes sentient life forms from other biological entities. Similarly, the ability of a network to mimic learning enables the network to increase its accuracy towards the desired output.

> Learning is defined as the process of updating the internal representation of the system in response to external stimuli so that it can perform a specific task. This includes modifying the network architecture, which involves adjusting the weights of the links, pruning, or creating some connection links and changing the firing rules of the individual neurons. (Schalkoff, 1997, p. 128)

ANNs would thus learn through an iterative process by examining the error term generated by the previous network architecture, adapting future network architecture to minimize future error terms. This is like the way human beings learn and process information. An ANN is said to have learnt if it can (1) handle imprecise, fuzzy, noisy, and probabilistic information without noticeable adverse effects on response quality and (2) generalize from the tasks it has learnt to unknown ones (Basheer & Hajmeer, 2000).

Learning algorithms can either be supervised, unsupervised or a hybrid of both. In supervised learning, the input and expected output is provided to the network. The network is then expected to model the output, providing the closest approximation between the actual and modelled output. Specifically, the use of supervised learning reproduces the characteristics of a certain (unknown) relationship between the input and output data. In contrast, unsupervised learning provides the input and output data, but not the relationship between them. The network is then expected to minimize the cost function (the error term) by determining that relationship that links the input to the output data. At each training iteration the network produces a result that is then used to update the weights of the neurons. These weights are continually updated until the minimal cost result is achieved.

As per Haykin (1994) and Hassoun (1995), there are four basic learning algorithms. Error-correction learning (ECL) is used in supervised learning in which the arithmetic difference (error) between the ANN solution at any stage during training and the corresponding correct answer is used to modify the connection weights so that the overall network error is gradually reduced. The most popular learning algorithm used in ECL is the backpropagation (BP) algorithm. As a precursor to the BP algorithm, the gradient descent method is used to minimize the error function through updating the weights of the neurons. The method finds the gradient of the weight space and selects the steepest descent at each iteration, finding either a minimum or infinitely decreasing path. When the minimum is found, it is not necessary the global minimum, which can incorrectly lead to premature stopping of the training of the network. The BP algorithm avoids this pitfall by introducing two more parameters (the learning rate and the momentum parameter) that affect the speed at which the system learns. These parameters force the search to consider results from previous iterations, thereby avoiding the search from finding a local minimum or infinitely decreasing path. This "consideration" is what gives the algorithm its name as it passes information from each output back to the input and hidden layers of the network.

The Boltzmann learning (BL) rule (Hinton & Sejnowski, 1983) is a stochastic rule derived from thermodynamic principles and information theory (Anderson & Rosenfield, 1988). It is like ECL however each neuron generates an output based on a Boltzmann statistical distribution (Jain et al., 1996) that renders learning extremely slower.

The Hebbian learning (HL) rule by Hebb (1949) is based on neurobiological experiments that postulate that: "if neurons on both sides of the synapse are activated synchronously and repeatedly, the synapse's strength is selectively increased." Perhaps one of the oldest learning algorithms, the algorithm is a reasonable proxy for biological learning methods, making it ideal in systems where the focus is on the activation of neurons in a particular location as opposed to over the entire network. Unlike ECL and BL, learning is done locally by adjusting the synapse weight based on the activities of the neurons.

In the competitive learning (CL) rule, all neurons are forced to compete amongst themselves such that only one neuron will be activated during any given iteration with all the weights attached to it adjusted (Jain *et al.*, 1996). CL is useful for classifying input data into a discrete set of output classes through a particular CL algorithm, vector quantization (VQ). In VQ, those neurons that closely match the input are regarded as the best matching unit, making all neighboring neurons to be readjusted to be closer to the input data. This enables the neurons to become detectors of individual features, with a combination of feature detectors being used to identify large classes of features from the input data—much the same principle observed in a SOM.

BUILDING AN ANN IN FINANCE

As neural networks can be used to model non-linear relationships, they can be used to model the behavior of agents within financial markets. Specifically, if one can predict future share prices, then not only does a profit opportunity exist, but the validity of market efficiency can be questioned. The creation of a neural network is achieved through three phases.

Neural Network Modelling

Enke and Thawornwong (2004) select a feed-forward neural network with a sigmoid hyperbolic tangent function as the activation function. This function generates an even distribution over the input values. A single hidden layer was also chosen since Swales and Yoon (1992) show that it has been successfully used in financial classification and prediction. Each relevant input variable was assigned to a separate neuron within the input layer using the *n-fold* cross validation technique. The authors used the network to predict the direction of share prices, thus there were two output neurons in the output layer. The back-propagation algorithm was used to train the network and the input data was normalized to minimize any effect of magnitude among the inputs. Using the RMSE criterion, the authors found the best network architecture in terms of the number of hidden layers and neurons within each layer. A backward stepwise regression for dimensionality reduction was employed to assume a linear additive relationship for the classical linear regressions. The least significant variable was removed iteratively until all remaining variables are significant. The neural network is assessed using out-of-sample data using traditional measures, such as RMSE. However, as suggested by Pesaran and Timmermann (1995), traditional performance measures may not be strongly related to profits from trading—a statistically significant result in predicting share prices could be eliminated when one decides to create an investment strategy from these results, incurring transaction costs in the process. Thus, an alternative approach is to look at the proportion of correctly predicted signs of share returns as this is agnostic of transaction costs and does not infer any profit-making initiative on the part of the investor.

Training a Neural Network

A neural network is only as accurate as the data used in training it. The learning environment (data inputs) of the network is thus a crucial component in building a network. Once data has been sourced and processed (if necessary), then one decides on the learning algorithm.

Most literature relies on a neural network to generate buy or sell signals. The data used can range from raw data (such as volume, price or change in price) to derived data (such as technical or fundamental indicators). During the training phase, the network is at risk of being either over-trained (implying that it cannot generalize to out-of-sample data) or under-trained (fails to achieve the desired output out-of-sample). Over-training can occur when either too many hidden nodes exist or too many time periods are used, a problem that can be solved by using a test and train procedure (Lawrence, 1997). The procedure would require the network to be trained using a set percentage of the data (say 90%) and tested on the remaining proportion. Performance of the network can be easily detected and the network configuration or learning algorithm can be changed accordingly. Thus, over training of a network can be controlled by the experimenter.

While it is ideal to have voluminous amounts of data to use in building the network, the practical consideration of computer processing power and speed needs to be considered. Poor results can be due to insufficient processing capacity. The most common network architecture used in financial neural networks is a multilayer feed-forward network trained using back-propagation (Lawrence, 1997). Back-propagation passes errors through the network from the output layer towards the input layer. As the output layer is the only layer that has a target value, errors are backpropagated from previous layers that in turn change the connection weights. The activation used is also dependent on what data is being learned. For example, the sigmoid function works best when learning about average behavior (Klimasauskas, 1993) while the hyperbolic tangent function works best when learning about deviation from the average. While the back-propagation algorithm can be used in feed-forward neural networks, Ngiam et al. (2011) argue that gradient descent learning (specifically the stochastic gradient descent (SGD) method) can be used to train a recurrent neural network. The SGD method easy to implement over a large data set but requires much input from the researcher to optimize the learning rates and convergence criteria. Regardless of the learning algorithm used, financial neural networks are sensitive to over-training. Thus, validation techniques such as those discussed above need to be employed.

Network Organization

While back-propagation network architecture is the most common for financial networks, other types have been used successfully. Examples of these will be discussed below.

The back-propagation network is the most used as it is generally easy to implement and offers good generalization abilities. When trained appropriately (which can be problematic given the optimal network configuration and parameters), these networks offer high levels of performance. The use of genetic algorithms with back-propagation networks is useful when the input dimensionality is large.

Recurrent network architecture is based on the underlying assumption of patterns repeating over time. Specifically, the connection between the neurons and layers form a directed cycle, in that an internal state is created allowing the network to exhibit dynamic temporal behavior. If the network (or layers within the network) can remember previous outputs, there is a greater success rate in determining time-dependent patterns. These networks also offer reasonably good performance.

The self-organizing network architecture of Wilson (1994) was designed to construct a non-linear chaotic model of share prices from volume and price data. It provides an advantage over other network architectures as it reduces the number of hidden nodes required for pattern classification as well as develops the network organization automatically during training. A (significant) drawback was that, at the time, overfitting and training were problematic in achieving good performance. While algorithms have developed since, it is still a function of the researcher to investigate the performance of the Self Organizing Map (SOM) (or any neural network) to ensure tractability in the results.

A final category of network organization is that of hybrid architectures. Any neural network that combines any of the above or other information processing techniques would fall into this category. Often, combining more than one type of architecture can result in superior performance. For example, the combination of a neural network with an expert system would not only predict future prices, but also generate signals to buy or sell the share. The expert system would validate the output of the neural network, training it to be more accurate. However, as (any) expert system is designed by the experimenter, it suffers from the biases and decision-making processes that they contribute.

Network Performance

The performance of neural network is often measured on its ability to predict output data (in this case, share) prices. Ideally, the network should offer superior performance relative to other statistical methods. One can apply various time series models to that of share price data and determine which provides the best fit.

CASE STUDY

Standard Bank plugs into Watson

October 27, 2014

Following Metropolitan Health's announcement of the first commercial application of IBM's Watson technology in Africa, Standard Bank has revealed it will become the first financial institution on the African continent to implement it.

Watson breaks traditional barriers in computing by embracing artificial intelligence, natural language processing and dynamic learning when assisting customers and businesses with the interpretation of data.

The agreement will see Standard Bank South Africa partnering with IBM in assessing the product.

Although the IBM Watson program has been used for other applications, notably in the healthcare arena, it will be the first time in the Middle East and Africa that this technology will be used by a bank to interpret and maximize use of our data," says Vuyo Mpako, Head of Innovation & Channel Design at Standard Bank. "The ultimate beneficiaries of the project will be our customers for whom the process-known as 'cognitive computing' will undoubtedly bring many benefits as we continue to identify innovative ways of doing business and build a bank for the future.

The agreement with IBM is part of our commitment to seeking out and introducing innovative technologies that not only broaden our capabilities, but also have the potential to change the way we see banking and the way our customers interact and are serviced by us.

At the heart of the system is the efficient identification, gathering and use of customer information in a matter of seconds-thereby enabling the user to accurately assess a customer's requirements and respond to his or her needs.

Our partnership with IBM is without doubt one of the most important and potentially beneficial projects ever to have been undertaken in the banking arena on the African continent.

Piloting Watson is about doing the right things better and taking a major step in our commitment to provide banking services and solutions that are built around our customers and offer enhanced banking experiences. This will be achieved through the benefits that Watson offers in consolidating data and improving service levels and accuracy," says Mr Mpako.

https://gadget.co.za/standard-bank-plugs-into-watson/

QUESTIONS

1. How does one find the optimal parameters for an ANN?
2. How often should one change the optimal parameters in an ANN?
3. Should you outsource the development of an ANN for your organization? What are the advantages and disadvantages of this approach?

CHAPTER 7

MANAGING ANALYTICAL PROJECTS

LEARNING OBJECTIVES

After reading this chapter you should be able to:

- Appreciate that data science does not start with building a model
- Appreciate and understand the elements of the model development life-cycle

FOUR LENSES TO EVALUATE DATA SCIENCE PROBLEMS

Aspiring (and current) data scientists are most often those who enjoy complex problems to solve, often in pursuit of the truth as told by data than any business objective. However, in the workplace, it is difficult for data scientists to ascertain which projects they should focus on, along with criteria on which these projects should be evaluated. While a "true" data scientist is one who pursues the truth, this must be tempered with the practicalities of running a business. It is imperative for data scientists to be both action-oriented and insights-oriented, as one without the other is a recipe for disaster.

A Primer on Business Analytics: Perspectives from the Financial Services Industry, pages 103–111.

One can ask the following questions when determining which projects to focus time and effort on. All these questions are closely linked to how a postgraduate student will conduct research for academic purposes. Recall that any research would effectively require five core chapters—an Introduction, a Literature Review, Data and Methodology, a presentation and discussion of results, and a Conclusion. If you were to treat your data science project with this lens, it helps to introduce academic rigor into the data science lifecycle.

Lens 1. Objectives vs Questions vs Hypotheses

The challenge facing data scientists today is that we often do not dig deeper into surface level insights. Observation should be conducted with the rigor of scientific inquiry, yet few treat it that way. Data scientists need to contextualize their projects using terms sourced from academic research—objectives, problems, and hypotheses. From an academic perspective, the objective speaks to the aim and purpose of the work. It is meant to be succinct, yet broad enough to fit on a billboard (this helps get to the point rather quickly and is ironically difficult for numbers-oriented people to do!). Objectives have verbs associated with them and can be stated in general terms. Objectives are normally understood by the layperson.

Problems or questions are meant to specify more detail than your objectives. They help to define the scope of the study. In most instances, problems need to be solved and thus are posed in a question format. At this point of enquiry, it is important to note that these questions may not be empirically testable.

The last elements to define are the hypotheses. These are specific, clear, and testable propositions or predictive statements about the possible outcome. They are also tested empirically. Hypotheses are in effect assumptions that you wish to validate via data science methods. Recall from your research methodology course that a hypothesis often has a null (default statement) and an alternative. You would then rely on statistical tests (which produce a p-value) to determine whether you reject or fail to reject the null hypothesis. Notice that the opposite of rejecting the null hypothesis is not to accept it! A null hypothesis can never be accepted, as it is based on probabilities, which are rarely (never) equal to 0 or 1!

Lens 2. Which Tool Should I Use?

It's human nature to complicate things, more so for data scientists. Data scientists can sometimes make mountains out of molehills, especially when finding the best tool or algorithm to solve a problem. We sometimes use the most advanced techniques without really understanding the context of use of each specific algorithm. It is true that algorithms developed over the years are meant to be an improvement over previous generations (for example, recall from previous chapters that machine learning is meant to enhance the shortcomings of certain statistical methods). However, many times data scientists are attracted to the latest technique, without really knowing what came before it or why it was developed in the first place. It is important to realize that simpler solutions are always preferred over their counterparts. This line of thinking is linked quite closely to risk-based approaches.

This is embodied in Occam's Razor. When presented with two explanations for the same problem, where both account for all the facts, the simpler one is more likely to be correct. Remembering the beauty of simplicity goes a long way in making a successful data science project to be implemented—there is no point in using a machine learning algorithm to predict something on a daily basis, if no one can action that output on a daily basis. Similarly, if a logistic regression produces equally robust output as a neural network, the logistic regression is preferred.

In summary, when picking between mathematics, statistics, and computer science methods, consider the theory and data on your topic.

Lens 3. Playing for Fun vs Playing to Win

A data scientist is inherently a person with a passion for numbers and a curiosity for uncovering the "secrets" held in data. Often, this "whimsical" nature can lead a data scientist to focus on perfection as opposed to practicality, simply because the perfection allows him or her to spend hours over analysis instead of striking a balance between analysis and action. It is imperative to strike a balance between data experimentation and business objectives. This is where academia sometimes falls short—in the search for the perfect answer, many academics spend their lives in pursuit of some holy grail that is unattainable (and if it is, it remains in the theoretical realm as opposed to the practical realm). The successful data scientist needs to produce answers that are logical and can "stand trial." Running a business is not only learnt from academic textbooks—there are complex relationships at play, exogenous factors at play, and often "hidden hands" at play that make prediction in the face of uncertainty, volatility, ambiguity and complexity extremely difficult.

Lens 4. Distinguishing Between Actions and Insights

Linked to the previous lens, the practicality of the output needs to be weighed. In a similar fashion to Occam's razor, the "equivalent" in the business world is to simply weigh the costs and benefits of the project (in monetary terms). There are too many examples of data science projects that provide insights, but do not lead to any action. Don't get me wrong—there is a place for projects that involve a large element of reporting or simply insights that define strategy. Those are in demand and will still be in demand. However, the organization needs to have both initiatives.

One example of a cost would be your time (and salary) in relation to what another project you could have focused on. Benefits would only be realized if someone executes on the output of your project. This execution is typically done

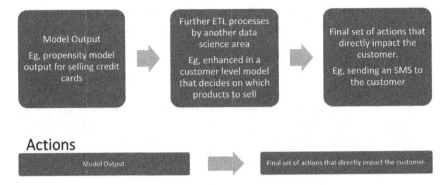

FIGURE 7.1. The Difference Between Insights and Actions (Source: The Author)

by those in the front office. This then derives value for the project and ultimately the organization.

What is the difference between insights and actions? Consider Figure 7.1. Insights are generated from some model. They are then further processed to generate actions. Those actions are what directly impact the customer. Actions are therefore those set of decisions that the customer needs to make. Insights, in contrast, are provided to another (internal) area in the organization for further processing.

BALANCING DATA SCIENCE EXPERIMENTATION WITH BUSINESS OUTCOMES

Data science and experimentation are typically seen as two sides of the same business coin. While this is true to a certain extent, it's a simplistic view that overlooks several important nuances in the relationship between the two. The most significant of these is the fact that experimentation within the realm of analytics can be harnessed in two quite distinct ways depending on what business outcomes are desired.

Of course, when the primary desired business outcome is a greater sense of understanding and stability in a highly uncertain operating environment, such as the one created by Covid-19, the value of both of these main forms of data science experimentation is highlighted.

The first level of experimentation takes place within the realm of analytics itself and is applied by a data scientist to find answers to specific questions or problems. This could be referred to as the 'exploration' variety of analytics experimentation. Then there is a second form of experimentation, which is also undertaken by the data scientist, but is not aimed at answering a specific question. Rather it is a form of experimentation that could be referred to as 'prospecting,' and it requires that the data scientist be given at least a measure of freedom or empowerment in order to 'dig around in the data' and see if anything of value emerges. Of course, as with any type of prospecting, there's a good chance that this type of experimentation does not deliver any results that are of significance to the business. At the worst, it might help to identify actions that should be avoided; and at the best, it could uncover the next massive vein of business gold that could be mined by the organization for many years to come.

The obvious problem with this second form of 'prospecting' experimentation is that the potential for a significant return on investment is limited. Which is why most companies are understandably unsure about throwing money at it. After all, in a challenging environment, where success at cost cutting has become a key performance indicator, it's already difficult to justify the often-high salaries paid to data scientists due to pure supply and demand dynamics. And adding a layer of experimentation to their job description can make it even more difficult to fully quantify the bottom-line value, if any, that they add. So, it's understandable that some businesses are reticent to make such an investment that offers no real guarantee of generating significant returns.

In contrast, most companies are quite comfortable with their data scientists spending a good amount of their work time using experiments to explore solutions to clearly defined problems. Especially since this type of work has clarity on expected outputs and places a measure of accountability on the data scientist for delivering the best solution in the end. However, the mind of your average data scientist is wired for creativity, discovery, and prospecting experimentation. It is what they are taught to do for many years while acquiring their university degrees. So, when an organization is unwilling to give them the freedom, at least for some of their working day, to do such prospecting, there's a very good chance that they will quickly move on to an employer that will. What's more, by preventing data scientists from using their science and skills to do these types of general experiments, a business could very well be missing out on identifying the next big idea or opportunity that could propel it to massive success, or at least, significant competitive advantage.

So, as is the case with so many sound business strategies, balance is key. While data scientists undoubtedly need to earn their keep by finding solutions to identified business problems, they also must be given the room to conduct experiments that may, or may not, achieve outcomes that are of any real value to the business. Achieving such balance is usually a product of a clear understanding of the fact that, within any business environment, the sought-after culture of innovation is a combination of disruption and optimization. As such, the data analytics function must exist and operate in close alignment with the business with a clear view of its strategy and desired outcomes. At the same time, the analysis of data must be given permission to be disruptive. The ratio of such a disruption focuses on relation to business-needs driven outcomes will differ from business to business, and is usually a function of various factors, particularly the size, budget, and maturity of the organization.

At the same time, the potential value of any level of 'prospecting experimentation' will always be directly proportional to the extent to which the data analytics function is given a voice in the business. So, even if you are a forward-thinking company with the budget to allow your data scientists to spend as much as 50% of their work time doing such blue-sky experimentation, if you are not willing to give them the opportunity to discuss their findings at an executive level, and really invest in understanding those findings, there's every chance that you'll be wasting their time and your money.

But if a business is willing to invest in the infrastructure, allow its data analysts the time and freedom to experiment, and bridge the often wide communication gap that exists between data science and business strategy, the potential exists that it could reap significant returns, and even become an industry game changer. And even if it doesn't, empowering data scientists to do what they do best, will almost certainly open the door to enhanced strategic thinking, which may well translate to diversified income streams across the organization's full value chain. Which, today, is a vital ingredient for business sustainability and certainly worth the investment.

Covid-19 has reinforced the importance and value of both types of data science experimentation. The pandemic represents a situation in which businesses are required to find solutions to problems they have never encountered before, and for which little to no historical data existed. In many cases, even identifying the specific problems that needs solving is challenging, let alone coming up with solutions to them. In this type of unknown scenario, prospecting and exploration really are your only viable options; and this has meant that organizations which had already recognized the importance of giving their data scientists the freedom to experiment went into the Covid-19 crisis with a relatively healthy advantage and could well emerge from the crisis with something of a head start on competition in the post-Covid-19 world.

THE MODEL DEVELOPMENT LIFE CYCLE

Whether you have a team of data scientists, have a universe of data to use or have the best software and hardware available, it is necessary to introduce project management principles into the development of models and corresponding "data products" (the outputs of models). First, let me highlight that a model is simply a set of rules, equations or functions that are sourced from mathematics, statistics, or computer science. Something as "simple" as an "IF THEN" rule can be considered a model (although a simple one).

Principle 1: All model rules must be documented. Whether for posterity, compliance or handover to other areas, rules must be documented in something that is not a piece of code.

Principle 2: Ensure correct definitions of the business objective and business problem. Hypotheses can change as the project commences.

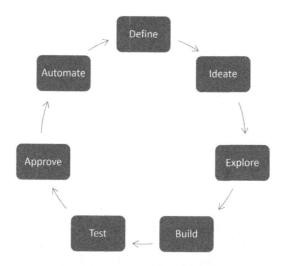

FIGURE 7.2. Model Development Lifecycle (Source: The Author)

Principle 3: Ensure enough time is dedicated to translating the objectives and problems into hypotheses that can be tested. Thereafter, assess feasibility of the problem with the data and tools at hand.

Principle 4: Track progress of the project and tread the fine line of over-promising and under-delivering. Sometimes in the search for perfection, data scientists are after a perfect answer as opposed to an answer that solves the immediate need and can be iterated in future phases.

Principle 5: Raise awareness of the initiative, its value, and celebrate milestones.

Principle 6: Ensure the process is governed and is compliant with relevant legislation.

Principle 7: Automate what can be automated—the model should never remain in a laboratory environment if it's in use. It should be moved to a production environment along with the necessary controls to measure and manage quality.

Given the above principles, a typical development lifecycle will comprise of the phases (Figure 7.2).

THE DATA AND ANALYTICS MATURITY CURVE

Through the years of seeing businesses in any sector come and go, the power of data and analytics has certainly become an important variable in predicting success. As such, we can group each business into one of four stages of the Data & Analytics Maturity Curve.

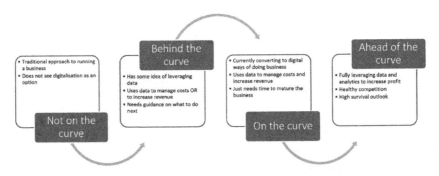

Figure 7.3. Categorization of business maturity in analytics (Source: The Author)

There are surprisingly businesses in each sector that still do not see the value of data and analytics in their daily operations. These are quite traditionalist in nature, seeing data (much less analytics) as something that is "not for them." It is impossible to imagine a single business that does not or can not run on data. While certain businesses certainly require a "human" element to operating, data is fundamental to the running of any business. The simplest example is preparing financial statements—that's data!

Next we have those businesses who are lagging their peer group. They have some idea of how to leverage data in their business operations, but need either assistance to do so or the push to do so. These businesses should start by using data to reduce any excess costs—by focusing on efficiencies in their business processes.

Third are the businesses that are on the D&A curve. They are the majority who are using some level of analytics in running their business and are particularly characterised as being "on," yet not "completely finished" with the digitisation of their business processes. These businesses are well on their way to continue surviving and perhaps thriving as their environment changes.

Finally, there are those who are ahead of the curve—who have disrupted their operations by leveraging data in ways that are not only new to their business, but also their industry. These businesses are currently thriving, but need to maintain the innovation momentum to ensure they do not lag as the rest of the industry catches up to them.

CASE STUDY

Discovery Bank is the first bank in South Africa to leverage behavioral insights to improve personal financial decisions. Read Hyland et al. (2021), who undertook a study to determine the extent to which the Discovery Bank business model is grounded in behavioral finance theory. The Discovery Bank business model was evaluated against the behavioral finance theoretical framework to establish the extent to which it conforms to behavioral finance theories. Behavioral finance research suggests that human biases can cause irrationalities that have a significant impact on decision making.

The authors find that the bank's business model is grounded in behavioral finance theory to a significant extent, with emphasis on modifying the behaviors that inhibit financial well-being. The bank generally uses incentives rather than nudges as behavior modification tools. For more information, visit the Discovery Bank website (www.discovery.co.za)

QUESTIONS

1. What happens if my hypothesis (question/objective) is wrong? Are they all equally damaging if wrong?
2. What happens if I use a more sophisticated method in answering my question?
3. Why is it important to prioritize work for my employer?
4. Is there ever time to have fun by exploring what's in the data? If my entire workday is billed per hour, do I even have time to experiment with data?
5. How do I create my hypotheses if my research question is not provided by the employer?
6. Can a hypothesis be created for qualitative/difficult to quantify research questions, such as those from behavioral finance?

CHAPTER 8

LEGAL, RISK AND COMPLIANCE CONSIDERATIONS IN DATA SCIENCE

LEARNING OBJECTIVES

After reading this chapter you should be able to:

- Have a basic knowledge of the ethical and philosophical use of data
- Appreciate the returns (and risks) that can be created from using and storing data

THE ETHICAL USE OF (BIG) DATA

With any technological advancement, it is often left to the ones who utilise said advancements to do so ethically and responsibly. While data science as a field and big data as an "object" can be used, so too must there be appropriate rules and regulations in place to ensure that constitutional rights of individuals are not violated. As such, many countries, beginning with those in Europe, have introduced data privacy and protection laws. These laws speak less to the amount of data collected, but rather what organisations can do with that data. There are two main

A Primer on Business Analytics: Perspectives from the Financial Services Industry,
pages 113–120.
Copyright © 2022 by Information Age Publishing

"pillars" of these laws—the gathering and storage of data; and the use of data. Organisations that collect data must do so safely and with participants providing informed consent. Orgnisations must then take measures to safely store and secure said data, prior to any use of it. When using this data, there is another distinction that should be made that relates to modelling of data and it's corresponding output. As most data science techniques rely on large datasets, the issue of one specific individual's data is lower given the aggregated modelling that occurs. However, if a company were to act on the output of that model, it would require a customised/personalised approach to marketing, which inevitably speaks to indivdiual data points as opposed to aggregates. Take for example a simple propensity to take up a credit card. When the data scientist is building this propensity model, any customer who qualifies for credit will be used in the sample set. However, when the bank wishes to approach any customer to sell a credit card, they can only do so if the customer has given express permission to do so. In South Africa, the Protection of Personal Information Act (POPIA) was introduced in 2018 (although it came into effect in 2021) to provide a legal framework on data privacy and usage amongst South African companies.

While the appropriate regulations and policies are still relatively new to South Africa, other countries have evolved in their data privacy journey. In 2015, the United Nations (UN) appointed a Special Rapporteur on the Right to Privacy (SRP). The appointment was in response to the Snowden allegations, and work that was undertaken in their aftermath by the Human Rights Council. For movie enthusiasts, you should watch the movie by the same name, where Joseph Gordon-Levitt plays Edward Snowden, part hero, part traitor, part villain (and he migrates between them based purely on the viewer instead of his actions!). The movie is a great portrayal of how the same action can have a variety of responses. Snowden shared information with the media on the variety of surveillance programmes The SRP produced his first report in March 2016 and identified several key themes that require investigatory work under the SRP's mandate. One of these is Big Data and Open Data. In July 2016, at the SRP's Conference on Privacy, Personality, and Information Flows at the New York University Law School, one of the authors of the present article, David Watts, was appointed to lead this part of the SRP's mandate. His key task was to oversee and coordinate the production of a paper on the privacy implications of Big Data, and Open Data, for presentation to the UN General Assembly, and the UN Human Rights Council in late 2017. The lack of a definition of big data poses several conceptual problems for the Big Data theme—how do you go about determining risk when you don't really know what you are measuring or assessing?

The SRP has expressed reservations about Open Data. According to the Open Knowledge International Handbook, it is defined as "data that can be freely used, re-used and redistributed by anyone—subject only, at most, to the requirement to attribute and share alike,." Open Data has become a public sector article of faith over the last few years. The asserted policy basis for this is that "governments have a significant amount of data that can be published publicly. Where this data is made available in a machine-readable way, digital services can leverage it to support improved information and service delivery for users." At first sight Open Data sounds fine as a concept, a noble and altruistic approach to dealing with data as a common good, if not quite the "common heritage of mankind." Who could object to data sets being used and re-used to benefit various parts of society and eventually hopefully all of humanity? It is what you can do with Open Data that is of concern, especially when you deploy the power of data science methods on the data sets which may have been made publicly available thanks to Open Data policies.

This sparks the debate on where the limit can and should be to ensure that data is not used for nefarious purposes. There are many examples of data leaks that spring to mind, by companies in diverse sectors, that question not only the security standards of those storing data, but also the reason or potential reasons that could emanate from the use of such data.

RISKS AND CHALLENGES OF USING (BIG) DATA

While many financial services identify and are increasing the use of data and analytics in their organization, it is not without its challenges from both an operational and compliance point of view. Given that larger, older organizations have many departments, there is a significant risk that technology used in one department is not adopted in the other. It is imperative for data not to be siloed, as this not only damages customer experience, but also poses legal risks to the company as the customer can potentially have outdated information in a department, which could minimize losses in another. For example, if a business entity has not renewed their business registration (which is an annual event), that company is no longer "real" in the eyes of the law. Therefore, any relationship with that company is null and void. If the company were to default, the bank has no recourse on how to start collection and recovery procedures, as the company is non-existent. For one department to end their relationship with the business is only beneficial to that silo of the broader bank. Second, as banks move towards cloud services, the question of security and resulting privacy of information becomes paramount. Many media scandals of banks (and other companies outside of financial services) show that protection of data is of utmost importance. Third, the access to data within an organization must be governed by strict processes. While a certain department has access to sensitive information on a customer, that data is used by them for the purposes of continuing their relationship with that customer. For another area to use that sensitive information without the customer's permission is unethical and soon will be illegal (as POPIA becomes implemented). Fourth, if one considers the plethora of big data available, the same grounds of justified usage become questionable. Many smaller fintech companies that offer credit facilities use external data, such as social media, to determine the credit worthiness of a customer. While this is certainly innovative, it highlights that the regulation of credit grantors needs to adapt to the various data sources available. One might argue for (or against) the use of social media data in granting credit. It thus becomes both a legal conundrum alongside a data science one.

CONSENT TECHNOLOGIES

From a financial services perspective, the introduction and implementation of POPIA (or it's equivalents) forces companies to implement measures of collection and storage of customer consent. This relies on applying forms of digital rights management—a technology that fell into disrepute after the way it was used by the entertainment industry to "prop-up" its decaying business model—to personal information. Essentially, these approaches attach permissions to personal information, and enable automated negotiations between information subjects and information recipients about the collection and subsequent use and disclosure of the subjects' personal information. This type of approach has been advocated by Professor Alex Pentland of MIT, who has supported placing "the individual much more in charge of data that's about them." This is a major step in making Big Data safer and more transparent, as well as more liquid and available, because people can now choose to share data.

Banks in South Africa had an implementation deadline of 1 July 2021 for their POPIA compliant processes to be in place. This resulted in not just an urgent need to capture customer responses, but also a need to re-engineer how data is used across the organization. In the context of banking (where multiple regulations apply), POPIA would introduce a granular form of marketing consent—if the customer wishes the bank to market similar products to them, the customer can choose the corresponding products as well as corresponding means of communication. Prior to POPIA, the customer would opt in or opt out of marketing as a collective (inclusive of any product or means of communication). This simple change forced banks to change processes that collect customer data, store customer data, and ultimately use customer data. On the latter, POPIA also seeks to ascertain whether the data of the participant was used for legally justifiable means. In other words, if I gave my personal data to the bank for the purposes of taking up a loan, the bank had to justify using that same data for the cross-selling of other products. This forces a shift in culture—one where product suitability is not just a mixture of aggressive targets and sales tactics to one where customer propensity as well as consent are at the heart of any data driven exercise.

One of the consequences of POPIA is to ensure that data is stored (and destroyed) appropriately. This also made many an organization weary of the management of information (from records in physical form to those in electronic), as one has to keep a register of records that exist as well as certificates to prove that the data has been successfully destroyed. During the implementation phase of POPIA, the "governance" of data became forefront not just in the minds of executives, but across all data-related roles. This was much to the chagrin of companies who only had a squad of data scientists, as you're now adding a governance function onto that role (which is already ill-defined and often overworked due to a shortage of qualified individuals). The necessity of looking after a customer's wellbeing becomes forefront because of treating customers fairly.

The law is facing significant new challenges that should be discussed. Personalization (the use of services, information, and knowledge) in the Web of Data, create new unregulated contexts and scenarios. Some boundaries arise within emerging data markets. Others unfold under non-harmonized jurisdictions and rules, while other boundaries relate to safety and collective security. For example, one needs to consider how to deal with multi-national corporations that have diverse geographical (and corresponding legal) jurisdictions. Further, it remains a question of balancing citizens' rights to privacy and those of national security—there are many movies that spring to mind on this theme!

CASE STUDY

Amazon Scraps Secret AI Recruiting Tool That Showed Bias Against Women
SAN FRANCISCO (Reuters)—Amazon.com Inc's AMZN.O machine-learning specialists uncovered a big problem: their new recruiting engine did not like women.

The team had been building computer programs since 2014 to review job applicants' resumes with the aim of mechanizing the search for top talent, five people familiar with the effort told Reuters.

Automation has been key to Amazon's e-commerce dominance, be it inside warehouses or driving pricing decisions. The company's experimental hiring tool used artificial intelligence to give job candidates scores ranging from one to five stars—much like shopper's rate products on Amazon, some of the people said.

"Everyone wanted this holy grail," one of the people said. "They literally wanted it to be an engine where I'm going to give you 100 resumes, it will spit out the top five, and we'll hire those."

But by 2015, the company realized its new system was not rating candidates for software developer jobs and other technical posts in a gender-neutral way.

That is because Amazon's computer models were trained to vet applicants by observing patterns in resumes submitted to the company over a 10-year period. Most came from men, a reflection of male dominance across the tech industry. (For a graphic on gender breakdowns in tech, see: tmsnrt.rs/2OfPWoD)

In effect, Amazon's system taught itself that male candidates were preferable. Its penalized resumes that included the word "women's," as in "women's chess club captain." And its downgraded graduates of two all-women's colleges, according to people familiar with the matter. They did not specify the names of the schools. Amazon edited the programs to make them neutral to these terms. But that was no guarantee that the machines would not devise other ways of sorting candidates that could prove discriminatory, the people said.

The Seattle company ultimately disbanded the team by the start of last year because executives lost hope for the project, according to the people, who spoke on condition of anonymity. Amazon's recruiters looked at the recommendations generated by the tool when searching for new hires, but never relied solely on those rankings, they said.

Amazon declined to comment on the technology's challenges but said the tool "was never used by Amazon recruiters to evaluate candidates." The company did not elaborate further. It did not dispute that recruiters looked at the recommendations generated by the recruiting engine.

The company's experiment, which Reuters is first to report, offers a case study in the limitations of machine learning. It also serves as a lesson to the growing list of large companies including Hilton Worldwide Holdings Inc HLT.N and Goldman Sachs Group Inc GS. N that are looking to automate portions of the hiring process.

Some 55 percent of U.S. human resources managers said artificial intelligence, or AI, would be a regular part of their work within the next five years, according to a 2017 survey by talent software firm CareerBuilder.

Employers have long dreamed of harnessing technology to widen the hiring net and reduce reliance on subjective opinions of human recruiters. But computer scientists such as Nahar Shah, who teaches machine learning at Carnegie Mellon University, say there is still much work to do.

"How to ensure that the algorithm is fair, how to make sure the algorithm is really interpretable and explainable—that's still quite far off," he said.

Masculine Language
Amazon's experiment began at a pivotal moment for the world's largest online retailer. Machine learning was gaining traction in the technology world, thanks to a surge in low-cost computing power. And Amazon's Human Resources department was about to embark on a hiring spree: Since June 2015, the company's global headcount has more than tripled to 575,700 workers, regulatory filings show.

So, it set up a team in Amazon's Edinburgh engineering hub that grew to around a dozen people. Their goal was to develop AI that could rapidly crawl the web and spot candidate's worth recruiting, the people familiar with the matter said.

The group created 500 computer models focused on specific job functions and locations. They taught each to recognize some 50,000 terms that showed up on past candidates' resumes. The algorithms learned to assign little significance to skills that were common across IT applicants, such as the ability to write various computer codes, the people said.

Instead, the technology favored candidates who described themselves using verbs more commonly found on male engineers' resumes, such as "executed" and "captured," one person said.

Gender bias was not the only issue. Problems with the data that underpinned the models' judgments meant that unqualified candidates were often recommended for all manner of jobs, the people said. With the technology returning results almost at random, Amazon shut down the project, they said.

The Problem, or the Cure?

Other companies are forging ahead, underscoring the eagerness of employers to harness AI for hiring.

Kevin Parker, chief executive of HireVue, a startup near Salt Lake City, said automation is helping firms look beyond the same recruiting networks upon which they have long relied. His firm analyses candidates' speech and facial expressions in video interviews to reduce reliance on resumes.

"You weren't going back to the same old places; you weren't going back to just Ivy League schools," Parker said. His company's customers include Unilever PLC ULVR.L and Hilton.

Goldman Sachs has created its own resume analysis tool that tries to match candidates with the division where they would be the "best fit," the company said.

Microsoft Corp's MSFT.O LinkedIn, the world's largest professional network, has gone further. It offers employers algorithmic rankings of candidates based on their fit for job postings on its site.

Still, John Jersin, vice president of LinkedIn Talent Solutions, said the service is not a replacement for traditional recruiters.

"I certainly would not trust any AI system today to make a hiring decision on its own," he said. "The technology is just not ready yet."

Some activists say they are concerned about transparency in AI. The American Civil Liberties Union is currently challenging a law that allows criminal prosecution of researchers and journalists who test hiring websites' algorithms for discrimination.

"We are increasingly focusing on algorithmic fairness as an issue," said Rachel Goodman, a staff attorney with the Racial Justice Program at the ACLU.

Still, Goodman and other critics of AI acknowledged it could be exceedingly difficult to sue an employer over automated hiring; Job candidates might never know it was being used.

As for Amazon, the company managed to salvage some of what it learned from its failed AI experiment. It now uses a "much-watered down version" of the recruiting engine to help with some rudimentary chores, including culling duplicate candidate profiles from databases, one of the people familiar with the project said.

Another said a new team in Edinburgh has been formed to give automated employment screening another try, this time with a focus on diversity.

Reporting By Jeffrey Dastin in San Francisco; Editing by Jonathan Weber and Marla Dickerson

https://www.reuters.com/article/amazon-com-jobs-automation/insight-amazon-scraps-secret-ai-recruiting-tool-that-showed-bias-against-women-idINKCN1MK0AH?edition-redirect=in

QUESTIONS

1. What are the implications of using data unethically?
2. How does one regulate the ethical use of data?
3. Find three examples where a company used data unethically and discuss the consequences.
4. What is the dictionary definition, and mathematical definition, of bias?
5. How does bias enter AI?
6. How does one minimize bias when building AI?

CHAPTER 9

FINTECH

LEARNING OBJECTIVES

After reading this chapter you should be able to:

- Have an understanding of fintech and how it closely relates to data science
- Appreciate that some problems in financial data science can be solutions to help environmental and societal goals.

CONTEXTUALIZING FINTECH

Arner et al. (2015) mention that Financial Technology (Fintech) has been around (albeit in other forms) since 1838. As can be deduced, the notion of enhancing the operational efficiency or the disruptive capability of firms is a long established "truth" for businesses to survive and thrive. If you distil it into the fundamental components of endogenous and exogenous factors, you easily see how it becomes important for business owners to manage what they can control; and accommodate (mitigate) what they cannot. As a single business among many in a competitive market, your influence on the market is minimal. However, in a smaller market (such as a monopoly or oligopoly), your opinion matters. It is important to know where you stand to influence what you can.

A Primer on Business Analytics: Perspectives from the Financial Services Industry, pages 121–131.
Copyright © 2022 by Information Age Publishing

While investors are no doubt revising their expectations now that the bubble has burst, they are not ready to give up on demands for rapid, steady growth in the companies they fund. This need to find new markets or products is a huge challenge. (Bower & Christensen, 1995)

From an investor perspective, investors rationally and reasonably expect their investment returns to increase over time. This constant expectation forces businesses to find new means of increasing profit, which can either be through new revenue streams or fewer cost streams. However, the "bottom line" has evolved over the decades to incorporate not just the shareholder, but society at large.

Anti-globalization demonstrations have made it apparent that if corporate expansion is seen to come at the expense of the poor and the environment, it will encounter vigorous resistance. (Bower & Christensen, 1995)

The realm of stakeholders that a business owner must now consider expand not just to shareholders, but to citizens as well. This is in response to "social justice" reforms that ensure that businesses are not just capital making entities, but also have a concern for the environment, for society and for governance. Indeed, one of the biggest questions facing any entrepreneur is how innovation can simultaneously meet both their expectations and those of society.

WHAT IS INNOVATION

Generally, disruptive innovations were technologically straightforward, consisting of off-the-shelf components put together in a product architecture that was often simpler than prior approaches. They offered less of what customers in established markets wanted and so could rarely be initially employed there. They offered a different package of attributes valued only in emerging markets remote from, and unimportant to, the mainstream. (Bower & Christensen, 1995)

We are primed to think of innovation as something that has "never been done before." While this may be true, look a bit deeper into that statement. To invent something that has never been invented before, the fundamental driver of success is the impact of that invention on society. For those inventions with a low impact, they normally do not last long. One can view innovation as either improving some inefficiency or disrupting some market. Therefore, innovation can be decomposed into operational innovation (where increased efficiencies are realized) or disruptive innovation (where a new manner of service delivery or product creation is realized).

Read and discuss examples of disruptive innovation: There are great stories from Honda, Toyota and Sony, to name a few.

- https://www.manufacturingglobal.com/smart-manufacturing/nestle-introduces-flexible-simple-and-cost-effective-modular-factories

- https://www.forbes.com/sites/simonmainwaring/2018/11/13/purpose-in-action-how-toyota-is-driving-growth-innovation-and-impact/?sh=31da7b7847fb
- https://digital.hbs.edu/platform-digit/submission/sony-from-disruptor-to-disrupted/

Bower and Christensen (1995) further define the management of innovation versus the management of technology. Managing innovation refers to creating a culture and process for individual innovation processes to thrive (by ultimately positively impacting the profit line of the business). In contrast, management of technology is more operational in nature, where the purpose is to guide integration of technology across the various business units in the larger organization.

Disruptive innovations, such as the ones described above, usually have 3 primary advantages. First, they are usually cheaper from the perspective of the customer. Second, they are more accessible and third, they use an existing business model with structural cost advantages. These 3 benefits accelerate the adoption and success of the innovation increasing the satisfaction of both the customer and the business.

Disrupting the Pyramid

Given current income distributions across economies, there is a clarion call for innovations to impact a greater number of individuals. This "pyramid" shape of society naturally leads one to conclude that an innovation that positively changes the lives of those who are at the base of the pyramid naturally impact a greater number of individuals than those at the top. As a result, an associated term of

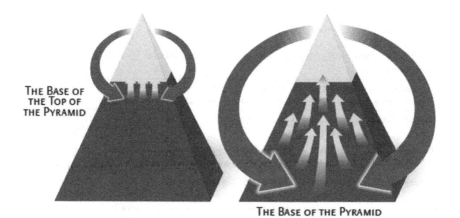

FIGURE 9.1.   Financial Inclusion (Hart & Christensen, 2002)

"financial inclusion" has emerged in recent years, which speaks to ensuring that all of society has access to basic banking facilities. By impacting the base of the pyramid, the long-term effects are a resultant shift of the entire pyramid into a higher standard of living. According to the World Bank, close to 1.7 billion adults remain unbanked as of 2020.

FINTECH

The new buzzword over the past 5 years has been the "rise of fintech" (Financial Technology). While more authoritative sources exist on this topic, it is important to obtain a basic understanding of this phrase in the context of analytics. Fintech refers to the digitization of the financial services industry—enabling products and services to be offered in an electronic or digital means to customers. This allows greater levels of service (by enabling faster interaction between the company and its customers), as well as allows the current lifestyle of customers to be incorporated into their financial services needs and interactions. The evolution of fintech, like the evolution of analytics, is not new. Table 9.1 from the Arner et al. (2017) book published by the CFA institute shows the 5 phases of the phrase. Companies initially serviced customers through a single customer channel, with decentralized systems and technology. As more channels of interaction became available, so too did the complexity in the volume and efficiency of said systems and technology. Today, we are used to reaching a bank via several channels, and also being "transferred" between channels. Furthermore, there is significantly more appetite from large banks to enlist the help of external companies to assist in enabling systems and technology to support the digital and customer-centric strategy adopted by most major banks.

TABLE 9.1. Evolution of the Digitalization of the Financial Services Industry (Alt & Puschmann, 2016)

Phases Characteristics	Phase 1: Until 1960	Phase 2: 1960–1980	Phase 3: 1980–2010	Phase 4: 2010–2020	Phase 5: From 2020
Strategy focus	Single customer channel	Two customer channels	Multi customer channels	Cross customer channels	Hybrid customer channels
Organization focus	Support processes	Back-office processes	Front-office processes	Provider processes	Customer processes
Systems focus	No systems integration	Partial internal systems integration	Internal systems integration	External financial services provider systems integration	External non-financial services provider systems integration

FINTECH IN SOUTH AFRICA

Many government-based institutions have embarked on a fintech journey, in response to the growing demand for a digitally focused economy that is beneficial for their citizens. Below is an excerpt from the South African government on its fintech vision, published in a white paper in 2020.

South Africa's fintech vision

...is vitally important for the SMME sector from opening new avenues to access finance and enterprise products that help in areas as diverse as cash-flow management to enhancing business and digital literacy. Supporting the development of fintechs provides an opportunity not only to solve for payment, credit and remittance problems, but also provide accessible and appropriate financial products such as investments, savings and insurance at scale.

At a national level, the focus in South Africa is on economic transformation, inclusive growth, and competitiveness. The 4th Industrial Revolution South Africa partnership (4IRSA)—an alliance between partners from the public and private sectors, academia and civil society launched by President Ramaphosa in 2019, reaffirms a national push towards promoting the digital economy for growth. Another important initiative is the development of the Intergovernmental Fintech Working Group (IFWG), formed in 2016, comprising representatives from the National Treasury (NT), South African Reserve Bank (SARB), Financial Sector Conduct Authority (FSCA), National Credit Regulator (NCR), Financial Intelligence Centre (FIC), and South African Revenue Service (SARS).

The above vision materializes four key components that are interlinked. To improve the overall wellbeing of South African citizens in a digitally based econ-

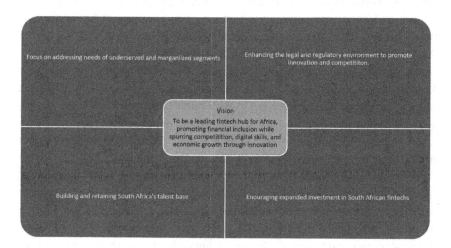

FIGURE 9.2.   South Africa's fintech vision (Source: Adapted by the Author)

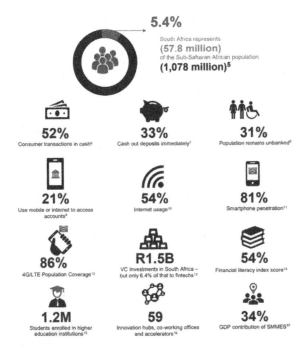

5.4%

South Africa represents
(57.8 million)
of the Sub-Saharan African population
(1,078 million)[5]

52%
Consumer transactions in cash[6]

33%
Cash out deposits immediately[7]

31%
Population remains unbanked[8]

21%
Use mobile or internet to access accounts[9]

54%
Internet usage[10]

81%
Smartphone penetration[11]

86%
4G/LTE Population Coverage[12]

R1.5B
VC Investments in South Africa – but only 6.4% of that to fintechs[13]

54%
Financial literacy index score[14]

1.2M
Students enrolled in higher education institutions[15]

59
Innovation hubs, co-working offices and accelerators[16]

34%
GDP contribution of SMMES[17]

FIGURE 9.3. Drivers of Fintech in South Africa (Source: South Africa Fintech Vision Report, 2020)

omy, it is crucial for relevant skills to be in supply (preferably by South Africans) as well as investment opportunities that create an exchange of knowledge between governments. All of this is underpinned by a sound regulatory framework that ensures that human rights and other legal considerations are maintained.

The current state of the South African digital economy shows that we have a long way to go before any tangible benefits can be realised through digitalisation. Indeed, the phrase "4IR," referring to the Fourth Industrial Revolution, has resulted in collaborative efforts between private and public sectors. Some statistics of the country are shown in Figure 9.3. First, there are still a significant number of South Africans who transact in cash. This, coupled with the low (21%) number who access their accounts digitally point toward a society that is still emerging as digital nation. The high number of unbanked citizens show the marked difference of financial inclusion in our country, but that is also lowered by a low number of citizens who know about financial literacy. The join problems of increasing financial literacy and increasing the population of those with a bank account make achieving successes from digitalisation a difficult journey.

CASE STUDY

10 Up-and-Coming South African Fintechs Shaping Financial Services Now
November 2020

A new generation of South African start-ups are leveraging emerging tech to boost inclusion across the financial services industry and lower the cost of transaction services for businesses.

The financial sector in Africa—which has a huge unbanked population and a young demographic hooked on mobile phones—is ripe for disruption, and a new generation of creative South African fintech start-ups is taking the lead in offering innovative services to enterprises and consumers alike.

The financial sector in Africa is responding to real-world conditions by offering services such as mobile banking, and various technologies that lower the cost of access to transaction services for enterprises. In 2019, African tech start-ups broke records. The African tech sector's attractiveness to investors is the highest it has ever been, with much of the interest being directed towards ventures within the financial services sector.

Financial inclusion secured the top spot when it comes to deal volume and value last year, with ventures that improve access to financial services being awarded over 54% of total investment, according to a report by Partech Partners. An investment summary report for 2019 from London-based research firm, Briter Bridges, also noted the trend, highlighting South Africa as one of the top investment regions.

Fintech is technology that is applied to financial services or the management of transaction operations in businesses. While a number of countries in sub-Saharan Africa, including most recently Mauritius, are trying to lay the foundation for a thriving fintech start-up scene, South Africa already has a number of fintech success stories. These include the likes of Yoco, Tyme Bank, Jumo and Luno. These brands are at a more advanced stage than other start-ups, having successfully partnered with big corporates, grown a large customer base, attracted big investments and challenged the industry status quo. But there are also a variety of smaller fintech ventures looking to grow.

Rand Merchant Bank's SA Fintech in Motion Report for 2019 outlines how digital innovations have fundamentally altered the way we communicate, transact and access information, spawning entirely new business models. And the opportunities that these forces are creating are set to shape the future of financial services.

According to Dominique Collett, a senior investment executive at Rand Merchant Investment Holdings (RMI) and the head of AlphaCode, an RMI incubation, acceleration and investment vehicle, South African fintechs are embracing emerging technology, social media and a changing consumer base to create new business models and change the financial services landscape.

"SA's financial services sector is undergoing a process of unprecedented change brought about by the disruptive impact of fintech challengers and the emerging technologies powering their business models," says PwC, the world's second-largest professional services firm."Fintechs are redrawing the competitive landscape and blurring the lines that define players in the financial services landscape."

Below is CIO Africa's top 10 list of up-and-coming fintech start-ups to watch—smaller than some of the more well-known financial services start-ups but making inroads into the consumer and enterprise markets with new mobile apps and innovative niche services.

Bank Zero
Year Founded: 2018
Headquarters: Johannesburg
CEO: Yatin Narsai

What they do: Bank Zero is SA's newest bank. It's an exclusively digital mutual bank that offers a mobile app and promises free basic banking with charges only for additional extras.

Competitors include: TymeBank and Discovery Bank
Customers: Both businesses and individuals.

Why they're a fintech start-up to watch: Bank Zero is South Africa's first digital-only bank. This fintech is the brainchild of venture capitalist and tech entrepreneur Michael Jordaan and banking innovator Yatin Narsai, who worked together to transform First National Bank into the most innovative bank in the world.

Mama Money
Year Founded: 2013
Headquarters: Cape Town
CEO: Co-founded by Mathieu Coquillon and Raphael Grojnowski.

What they do: Mama Money is a cross-border, money-transfer service allowing migrants to send money from South Africa to their home countries. Mama Money tackles the high cost of international money transfers and currently operates in 12 countries.

Competitors include: Meerkat and TransferGalaxy
Customers: Migrants keen to send money home to support their families.

Why they're a fintech start-up to watch: Earlier this year, Mama Money partnered with Western Union to allow customers to send money to their loved ones around the world via Western Union's Global Network.

LulaLend
Year Founded: 2014
Headquarters: Cape Town
CEO: Trevor Gosling

What they do: LulaLend makes use of proprietary credit scoring technology to provide quick decisions, fast funding, and transparent pricing to small and medium-size enterprises (SMEs).

Competitors include: Rainfin and JUMO
Customers: SMEs located in South Africa that have been in business for over a year with an annual revenue higher than 500,000ZAR (US$30,000).

Why they're a fintech start-up to watch: The B2B digital lender was recently recognized in the 2020 Inclusive Fintech Awards. The awards are given out to just 50 fintech start-ups from around the world that are trying to provide financial services to underserved communities.

Clickatell
Year Founded: 2000
Headquarters: Cape Town
CEO: Pieter de Villiers

What they do: A global player in mobile communications and chat commerce, Clickatell offers real-time customer engagement and transaction platforms designed to enable businesses to connect, engage and transact with their customers via mobile chat and other digital channels.

Competitors include: Infobip
Customers: Ranging from Fortune 500 organizations to well-known consumer brands and SMEs.

Why they're a fintech start-up to watch: The company has a well-established track record and has been in the business for two decades. Clickatell serves over 15 000 customers and has connected to six billion mobile phone users in over 220 countries and territories worldwide.

Livestock Wealth
Year Founded: 2015
Headquarters: Johannesburg
CEO: Ntuthuko Shezi

What they do: Livestock Wealth is a crowdfunding company that focuses on funding for cattle. The company connects investors with farmers that need funding using cattle as a form of investment.

Competitors include: SwiftVee
Customers: People with no access to the land, time or skills needed to own livestock and run a professionally managed farming operation; including big retailers like Woolworths.

Why they're a fintech start-up to watch: The livestock crowd farming platform recently expanded its offerings to include a shared farming project that buys, cares for, and sells free-range, grass-fed beef.

Paycode
Year Founded: 2014
Headquarters: Johannesburg
CEO: Ralph Pecker

What they do: Paycode provides financial service access to the unbanked by giving them a biometric identity. In doing so, the fintech is opening the world's financial systems to everyone.

Competitors include: Veridium
Customers: The unbanked living in the world's least developed markets.

Why they're a fintech start-up to watch: Like LulaLend, Paycode was also selected out of 403 applicants as a winner at the Inclusive Fintech 50 Awards for 2020. The fintech start-ups named on this year's list were chosen based on criteria including inclusiveness, innovation, scale potential and traction.

Bettr
Year Founded: 2015
Headquarters: Cape Town
CEO: Tobie van Zyl

What they do: Yet to officially launch, Bettr is building an alternative banking service for low cost, everyday transactional use. The digital banking app won't provide products but will adopt a marketplace business model to connect their user community with the products that best meet their needs.

Competitors include: Bank Zero, Tyme Bank
Customers: Aimed at tech-savvy Generation Z and millennial customers.

Why they're a fintech start-up to watch: A technology company that aims to do banking differently, Bettr's "marketplace" business model means that consumers will have access a range of products and services and don't have to pay various fees to transact with multiple different banks.

Peach Payments
Year Founded: 2011
Headquarters: Cape Town and Johannesburg
CEO: Rahul Jain

What they do: Peach Payments build online payments systems for Africa. The fintech allows businesses to accept payments via their websites and mobile apps.

Competitors include: PayU, Ozow
Customers: The payments platform is available for entrepreneurs, SMEs, and large enterprises in South Africa.

Why they're a fintech start-up to watch: The company currently services between 1,500 and 2,000 merchants—including three of South Africa's four big supermarket groups —and is signing up 200 to 300 new merchants every week. Peach Payments recently raised additional capital to fund their African expansion.

Lettuce
Year Founded: 2019
Headquarters: Offices in the UK and Cape Town, South Africa.
CEO: Simon Dingle

What they do: Providing an open banking hub, the app allows users to see all their assets in one place. The platform offers real time market data so it's possible to track your assets, no matter what you are or where they are.

Competitors include: 22seven
Customers: Described as an "investment tracker for people who hate spreadsheets."

Why they're a fintech start-up to watch: Looking ahead, the Lettuce team are building tools to allow users to automatically rebalance their investments and buy and sell assets.

The People's Fund
Year Founded: 2017
Headquarters: Johannesburg
CEO: Luyanda Jafta

What they do: The People's Fund is a purchase-order crowdfunding platform for businesses that have orders with government and enterprises but need capital to deliver on these orders. The platform allows everyday people to participate in the growth of entrepreneurs, which makes it easier for entrepreneurs to get access to funding.

Competitors include: Thundafund, Jumpstarter
Customers: The platform is exclusive to black-owned, innovative businesses.

Why they're a fintech start-up to watch: The fund attempts to fill a gap in the financing of SMEs, helping entrepreneurs to buy assets they need. The range of campaigns they support is diverse from funding hives for a bee-keeping company to buying a vehicle refrigeration system for a chopped vegetable delivery service.

https://www.cio.com/article/3588090/10-up-and-coming-south-africa-fintech-startups-shaping-financial-services.html?upd=1617022384217

QUESTIONS

1. Why should companies innovate?
2. What is the value of innovation? How do we measure it?
3. Should we always be innovating?
4. What are the consequences of a fintech driven firm?
5. What impact does fintech have on the economy? On society?

CHAPTER 10

THE FUTURE OF BIG DATA

WHAT THE EVOLUTION OF DATA ANALYTICS CAN TEACH US ABOUT BUSINESS SUCCESS

While data science has gained massive importance as a vital business tool in recent years, it's not exactly a new concept. Some date the beginnings of the formal analysis of data for business use back to the 19th century, with Frederick Winslow Taylor's time management exercises. Others argue that data analysis has been around for as long as businesses have existed, but it just went by a different descriptor, namely 'consulting.' And still others go even further back, claiming that the use of data, albeit not on the technological scale of today, can be traced to the early Egyptians, who used it to build the pyramids.

Irrespective of one's belief in the origins of data science, the rapid and massive evolution and broadening of the science, particularly over the past sixty years or so, is beyond question. The arrival of computers in the late 1960s was the primary catalyst for this rapid increase in evolutionary momentum. Then, as recently as 2005, the evolutionary process exploded with the advent of big data, enhanced data warehousing capabilities, and the Cloud.

As quickly as the software and hardware used in these analytics evolved, particularly in areas like artificial intelligence, robotics, and machine learning so too did their use, and possibly more significantly, the expectations of what they should

A Primer on Business Analytics: Perspectives from the Financial Services Industry,
pages 133–137.

be doing for businesses. For most businesses, those expectations also evolved from wanting to leverage data and analytics to improve efficiencies, to requiring the analysis and application of data to ensure a competitive advantage. Inevitably, this caused the evolution of data analysis to speed up exponentially, and analytical techniques developed to meet the expectations, giving rise to disciplines like predictive analytics, data visualization and machine learning. However, the pace at which actionable insights have been unlocked by such analysis has been a lot slower, mainly due to a lingering shortage of qualified and capable analysts, the prohibitively high costs of tools, resources, and infrastructure, and a lack of insight by many organizations into the real value of investing in the science to answer business questions and catalyze business growth.

Adding to this gap between potential and actual outcomes is the fact that recently we witnessed another step change in the rationale for data analytics in business. Unfortunately, this was a result of many organizations effectively bypassing the optimization potential of the science, simply to keep up with the proverbial Jones's, by automating as many business functions as possible, and building bigger and better robots.

The major problem with this was that, in their rush to show that they are doing things better than their competitors, many businesses lost sight of the real value of data and the science of analyzing it. Which is really to understand customers to add value to them. And in so doing, build more sustainable, robust, diversified and growth-oriented businesses.

Of course, data analytics can, and should, be a cornerstone of business success and growth going forward. But there are a number of checks and balances that every business needs to have in place to ensure that it doesn't get ahead of itself and focus more on being at the cusp of the ongoing evolution of data analytics, and less on unlocking its real value for them and their customers.

Be savvy about the roles you choose to automate. The initial rush to robotics was driven largely by a desire from businesses to build something so intelligent that it could automate even the most complex of processes. While automation can, and must, be harnessed to automate certain functions—like checking the accuracy of client data against existing information—trying to shoehorn total automation into areas that require creativity, subjectivity and empathy is an undertaking that's doomed to fail. These functions can most certainly be augmented by artificial intelligence, but we have a long way to go before robots are solely responsible for these roles.

Don't put the cart before the horse. Before you rush off to automate a process, build a robot or use machine learning, it's essential to make sure you have the data and analytics ability required to fuel that process and maximize its likelihood of success. The truth is that data science, in all its iterations, will always be in a process of evolution. To maximize the benefits of the science in business, we need to understand that evolutionary process and follow it, at least to some extent, ourselves. In other words, businesses must learn to walk before we try to run, irrespective of the urgency they perceive to exist to keep up with what their competitors are doing.

Don't disrupt for the sake of disruption (or because everyone else is doing it). Make no mistake, disruption in every industry is very real. The way businesses work is transforming right before our eyes. But the idea that you must be disruptive to be successful, or to compete with other organizations, is fundamentally flawed. Disruption alone doesn't ensure success. Rather, that requires optimization, transformation, and an ability to respond quickly to disruption when it happens.

Check your motivation. The socioeconomic challenges facing South Africa today mean that there has never been a greater imperative for businesses to be motivated by more than profit. The triple bottom line is more relevant and important than ever before in the history of business, which highlights the need to be purpose driven and motivated by societal needs. Investors know it.

As do shareholders. So, if businesses are approaching data analytics, disruption, and automation from a purely financial angle, they are out of alignment with all their stakeholders. And that is not conducive to survival, let alone long-term success. Ironically, the very nature of technological advancement has created something of a Catch 22 situation for businesses. These advances have served to democratize data, make its collection more effective, and make it accessible to analysts for the purpose of business development. However, these change catalysts are available to all businesses, which means that leveraging them for competitive advantage is becoming progressively more difficult.

The key to successfully leveraging data and enjoying the benefits of its ongoing analytics evolution therefore doesn't necessarily lie in striving to always be at the cutting edge, no matter the cost. Rather the business that will ultimately win through its analytical competitiveness is the one that stays clear of a 'first-at-all-costs' mindset and instead balances the science with non-technical success components, including a culture that embraces the human development potential of a data driven business.

POST-COVID-19 BUSINESS SUCCESS

Apart from the obvious impact of months of lockdown on business turnover and profitability, one of the biggest challenges that faced organizations during the first few months of Covid-19 was a complete lack of data. The world had never faced a situation quite like this and given the significant dependence of businesses on data for strategy development and decision making, most companies found themselves having to 'shoot from the hip' given that there was now a structural break in their data flows, and they had no access to any particularly relevant customer, industry or economic data to analyze and inform their decisions.

Nine months later, there is at least some data available, and the amount of it is growing quickly. Now, the question is, how can businesses best leverage the Covid-19-related data they have access to in a way that enhances their effectiveness and growth? Perhaps more importantly, businesses need to be considering how they can apply the available data to rethink the way they do business in an operating environment that is likely to be very different from what it was up until the end of 2019.

A good example of this is digitization. Irrespective of the industry in which any business operates, or the type of customers it serves, over the past few months, virtually every organization in the world has learnt some very valuable lessons about the need to digitize as many of its operations as possible. Covid-19 has also provided very useful lessons about the importance of tailoring the customer experience to what the customer wants or, at least, is most comfortable with. These are extremely valuable insights, and businesses would be well advised to recognize them as such, and thoroughly analyze them to plot their growth journeys in the months and years ahead.

South Africa's national lockdown forced a widespread strategic refocus for most businesses in the country. Most became almost exclusively focused on survival and avoiding loss, whether of money, customers, or staff. As the economy gradually grinds back into motion, that focus must change again; and most businesses now have the data they need to drive this shift from survival back to growth. For most organizations, that return to sustainable growth is unlikely to come about by simply going back to doing things the same way they were before the pandemic. The world is a different place now, and businesses need to think, strategies and operate differently to succeed in it.

Interestingly, one of the main lessons to come out of Covid-19 is that it is possible, and indeed essential, to constantly be critically assessing whether there are other ways of doing business, or at least leveraging your assets and brand equity, to expand your operations and grow your market.

Gyms are a case in point. Before Covid-19, few if any gyms had considered that there may be business opportunities in digitizing their offering. The gym business model was based, almost entirely, on getting feet through the door of a physical building. When Covid-19 struck, and social distancing regulations meant gyms were some of the businesses that were forced to stay closed for the longest time, the shortcomings of this model were laid bare. In order to survive, gyms had to quickly rethink their business models, and most realized that there were opportunities to continue operating online, in the process, keeping their brands top of mind, and even going some way towards meeting their contractual obligations to their members.

It would be folly for these gyms to simply cast these augmented member offerings aside now that they are once again able to open their doors. Especially given that it is bound to take some time for attendance numbers to rise to what they were last year. Instead, they have a unique opportunity to incorporate the crisis lessons and leverage the associated member behavior data to significantly enhance their customer value proposition going forward.

And this is where the Covid-19 data that businesses have been able to gather through the course of a very challenging 2020 has the potential to be a massive game changer for many of these organizations. But for this data to be such a growth catalyst, the perspective of businesses must change. Instead of approaching data analysis from a 'prevention of future loss' angle, in which they merely try to cope with the new normal, businesses need to invest time and resources into finding ways to leverage this valuable customer, employee and operational data to define that new normal for themselves—one that allows them to expand and enhance their operations to catalyze and secure maximum growth, success and, of course, resilience into the future.

IN CLOSING

Any individual with experience in financial markets knows that the future is never what it supposed to be. Predictions are difficult in financial markets, despite the large array of technologies and methodologies that strive to achieve them for profitable outcomes. More so is the outlook on data and analytics. What one says today is the future of tomorrow, quickly becomes the relics of yesterday. We are entering a time where digitalization is most certainly a reality, although it grows at different rates for different economies. With ever increasing technological innovation, more data is generated, and faster (and more accurate and most importantly safer) means of analyzing said data is fast becoming a competitive landscape. For businesses to survive and thrive in this data-driven world, it is necessary to remain true to the foundational concepts of running a business -minimizing costs and maximizing revenue. How those are achieved by data and analytics is the ambit of not just executives, but every employee in the organization. Fintech is no longer a "new buzzword" or a separate form of innovation—it's become synonymous with innovation in the financial sector. With the continuing rise of fintech, so too must individuals consider the ethical and legal aspects of using, storing, and collecting data. It must be to uplift the overall level of societal wellbeing, while not alienating individuals or businesses alike. That is what I prefer to define as the future of analytics -not focusing on the methods or tools, but rather the striving to achieve an outcome that benefits as many as possible.

REFERENCES

Aamodt, A., & Plaza, E. (1994). Case-based reasoning: Foundational issues, methodological variations, and system approaches. *AI communications, 7*(1), 39–59.

Akrimi, J. A., RahimAhmad, A., George, L. E., & Aziz, S. (2013). Review of artificial intelligence. *Int. J. Sci. Res, 2*(2), 487–505.

Alagidede, P., & Panagiotidis, T. (2009). Modelling stock returns in Africa's emerging equity markets. *International Review of Financial Analysis, 18*(1), 1–11.

Álvarez-Díaz, M., & Álvarez, A. (2005). Genetic multi-model composite forecast for non-linear prediction of exchange rates. *Empirical Economics, 30*(3), 643–663.

Anderson, J., & Rosenfield, E. (1988). *Neurocomputing: Foundations of research.* MIT Press.

Angus, J. (1991). *Criteria for choosing the best neural network: Part 1* (pp. 1–26). Naval Health Research Centre.

Arner, D. W., Barberis, J., & Buckley, R. P. (2015). The evolution of Fintech: A new post-crisis paradigm. *Geo. J. Int'l L., 47,* 1271.

Arner, D. W., Barberis, J., & Buckley, R. P. (2017). *FinTech and RegTech in a Nutshell, and the Future in a Sandbox.* CFA Institute Research Foundation.

Arrow, K. (1950). A difficulty in the concept of social welfare. *Journal of Political Economy,* 328–346.

ASCE Task Committee on Application of Artificial Neural Networks in Hydrology. (2000). Artificial neural networks in hydrology. I: Preliminary concepts. *Journal of Hydrologic Engineering, 5*(2), 115–123.

Balkin, S., & Ord, J. (2000). Automatic neural network modeling for univariate time series. *International Journal of Forecasting, 16,* 509–515.

A Primer on Business Analytics: Perspectives from the Financial Services Industry,
pages 139–145.

Basheer, I. (1998). *Neuromechanistic-based modeling and simulation of constitutive behavior of fine-grained soils.* PhD Thesis, Kansas State University.

Basheer, I. A., & Hajmeer, M. (2000). Artificial neural networks: Fundamentals, computing, design, and application. *Journal of Microbiological Methods, 43*(1), 3–31.

Baum, E., & Haussler, D. (1989). What size net gives valid generalizations? *Neural Computation, 1,* 151–160.

Bernatzi, S., & Thaler, R. (1995). Myopic loss aversion and the equity premium puzzle. *The Quarterly Journal of Economics, 110*(1), 73–92.

Bonga-Bonga, L., & Makakabule, M. (2010). Modelling stock returns on the South African Stock Exchange: A nonlinear approach. *European Journal of Economics, Finance and Administrative Sciences, 19,* 168–177.

Bouckaert, R. R. (2003, August). Choosing between two learning algorithms based on calibrated tests. *ICML, 3,* 51–58.

Bower, J. L., & Christensen, C. M. (1995). Disruptive technologies: Catching the wave. *Harvard Business Review, 43.*

Box, G., & Jenkins, G. (1970). *Time series analysis: Forecasting and control.* Holden Day.

Breslow, L. A., & Aha, D. W. (1997). Simplifying decision trees: A survey. *Knowledge engineering review, 12*(1), 1–40.

Brock, W., Lakonishok, J., & LeBaron, B. (1992). Simple technical trading rules and the stochastic properties of stock returns. *Journal of Finance, 47*(5), 1731–1764.

Brockett, P., Cooper, W., Golden, L., & Pitaktong, U. (1994). A neural network method for obtaining an early warning of insurer insolvency. *Journal of Risk and Insurance, 61*(3), 402–424.

Brown, R. (1963). *Smoothing, forecasting and prediction of discrete time series.* Prentice-Hall.

Casdagli, M. (1991). Nonlinear forecasting, chaos, and statistics. In L. Lam & V. Naroditsky (Eds.), *Modeling complex phenomena* (pp. 131–152). Springer-Verlag.

Ciprut, Jose V. (Ed.). (2009). *Indeterminacy: The mapped, the navigable, and the uncharted.* MIT Press.

Clements, M., Franses, P., & Swanson, N. (2004). Forecasting economic and financial time-series with non-linear models. *International Journal of Forecasting, 20,* 169–183.

Crammer, K., & Singer, Y. (2002). On the learnability and design of output codes for multiclass problems. *Machine learning, 47*(2), 201–233.

Cristianini, N., & Shawe-Taylor, J. (2000). *An introduction to support vector machines and other kernel-based learning methods.* Cambridge University Press.

De Gooijer, J., & Hyndman, R. (2006). 25 years of time series forecasting. *International Journal of Forecasting, 22*(3), 443–473.

De Gooijer, J. G., & Kumar, V. (1992). Some recent developments in non-linear time series modelling, testing, and forecasting. *International Journal of Forecasting,* 135–156.

Delen, D., & Ram, S. (2018). Research challenges and opportunities in business analytics. *Journal of Business Analytics, 1*(1), 2–12.

Demuth, H., & Beale, M. (1998). *Neural network toolbox for use with MATLAB: User's guide; Computation, visualization, programming.* MathWorks Incorporated.

Desai, V. S., & Bharati, R. (1998). The efficacy of neural networks in predicting returns on stock and bond indices. *Decision Sciences, 29*(2), 405–423.

Elomaa, T. (1999, August). The biases of decision tree pruning strategies. In *International symposium on intelligent data analysis* (pp. 63–74). Springer.

Engle, R. (1982). Autoregressive conditional heteroscedasticity with estimates of variance of the United Kingdom inflation. *Econometrica, 50*, 987–1008.

Engle, R., & Ng, V. (1993). Measuring and testing the impact of news on volatility. *The Journal of Finance, 48*, 1749–1778.

Enke, D., & Thawornwong, S. (2004). The adaptive selection of financial and economic variables for use with artificial neural networks. *Neurocomputing, 56*, 205–232.

Fahlman, S. (1988). *An empirical study of learning speed in backpropagation.* Technical Report, CMU-CS-88-162.

Fu, L. (1995). *Neural networks in computer intelligence.* McGraw-Hill.

Fulton, S. L., & Pepe, C. O. (1990). An introduction to model-based reasoning. *PC AL* (January), 48–55.

Garth, A., Rollins, D., Zhu, J., & Chen, V. (1996). Evaluation of model discrimination techniques in artificial neural networks with application to grain drying. *Artificial Neural Networks in Engineering, 6*, 939–950.

Ghiassi, M., Saidane, H., & Zimbra, D. (2005). A dynamic artificial neural network model for forecasting series events. *International Journal of Forecasting, 21*, 341–362.

Graham, B., & Dodd, D. (1934). *Security analysis: Principle and technique.* McGraw Hill.

Granger, C. (1991). Developments in nonlinear analysis of economic series. *Scandinavian Journal of Economics, 93*(2), 263–276.

Hamilton, J. (1989). A new approach to economic analysis of nonstationary time series and the business cycle. *Econometrica, 57*, 357–384.

Harrison, J., & Kreps, D. (1978). Speculative investor behavior in a stock market with heterogeneous expectations. *The Quarterly Journal of Economics, 92*(2), 323–336.

Hart, S. L., & Christensen, C. M. (2002). The great leap: Driving innovation from the base of the pyramid. *MIT Sloan Management Review, 44*(1), 51.

Hassoun, M. (1995). *Fundamentals of artificial neural networks.* MIT Press.

Haykin, S. (1994). *Neural networks: A comprehensive foundation.* Macmillan.

Hebb, D. (1949). *The organisation of behaviour.* Wiley.

Hecht-Nielsen, R. (1988). Applications of counterpropagation networks. *Neural Networks, 1*, 131–139.

Hill, T., Marquez, L., O'Connor, M., & Remus, W. (1994). Artificial neural network models for forecasting and decision making. *International Journal of Forecasting, 10*(1), 5–15.

Hinton, G. E., & Sejnowski, T. J. (1983, June). Optimal perceptual inference. In *Proceedings of the IEEE conference on computer vision and pattern recognition* (vol. 448). IEEE.

Holt, C. (1958). Forecasting seasonals and trends by exponentially weighted averages. *International Journal of Forecasting, 20*, 5–13.

Hopfield, J. J. (1984). Neurons with graded response have collective computational properties like those of two-state neurons. *Proceedings of the national academy of sciences, 81*(10), 3088–3092.

Hutchinson, J., Lo, A., & Poggio, T. (1994). A nonparametric approach to pricing and hedging derivative securities via learning networks. *The Journal of Finance, 49*(3), 851–889.

Hyland, L. K., Sebastian, A., & Seetharam, Y. (2021). An application of behavioural finance in banking: The Discovery Bank Case, *Journal of Economic and Financial Sciences, 14*(1), a602.

Hyndman, R., Koehler, A., Ord, J., & Snyder, R. (2005). Prediction intervals for exponential smoothing state space models. *Journal of Forecasting, 24*, 17–37.

Hyndman, R., Koehler, A., Snyder, R., & Grose, S. (2002). A state space framework for automatic forecasting using exponential smoothing methods. *International Journal of Forecasting, 18*, 439–454.

Jadid, M., & Fairbairn, D. (1996). Predicting moment-curvature parameters from experimental data. *Engineering Applications of Artificial Intelligence, 9*(3), 309–319.

Jain, A. K., Mao, J., & Mohiuddin, K. M. (1996). Artificial neural networks: A tutorial. *Computer, 29*(3), 31–44.

Japkowicz, N., & Stephen, S. (2002). The class imbalance problem: A systematic study. *Intelligent Data Analysis, 6*(5), 429–449.

Kaboudan, M. A. (1999). A measure of time series' predictability using genetic programming applied to stock returns. *Journal of Forecasting, 18*(5), 345–357.

Kaiser, M. (1994). Time-delay neural networks for control. *IFAC Proceedings Volumes, 27*(14), 967–972.

Kanas, A. (2001). Neural network linear forecasts for stock returns. *International Journal of Finance and Economics, 6*(3), 245–254.

Kerber, R. (1992, July). Chimerge: Discretization of numeric attributes. In *Proceedings of the tenth national conference on Artificial intelligence* (pp. 123–128). Association for Computing Machinery.

Klimasauskas, C. C. (1993). Applying neural networks. *Neural Networks in Finance and Investing*, 47–72.

Kohonen, T. (1990). The self-organizing map. *Proceedings of the IEEE, 78*(9), 1464–1480.

Kolmogorov, A. (1941). Stationary sequences in Hilbert space. *Bulletin of Mathematics, University of Moscow, 2*(6), 1–40.

Kotsiantis, S. B., Zaharakis, I., & Pintelas, P. (2007). Supervised machine learning: A review of classification techniques. *Emerging artificial intelligence applications in computer engineering, 160*(1), 3–24.

Koza, J. R. (1992, December). Evolution of subsumption using genetic programming. In *Proceedings of the First European Conference on Artificial Life* (pp. 110–119). MIT Press.

Kuan, C., & Liu, T. (1995). Forecasting exchange rates using feedforward and recurrent neural networks. *Journal of Applied Econometrics, 10*(4), 347–364.

Kuo, C., & Reitsch, A. (1995). Neural networks vs conventional methods of forecasting. *The Journal of Business Forecasting*, 17–22.

Lawrence, R. (1997). Using neural networks to forecast stock market prices. *University of Manitoba, 333*, 2006–2013.

Lakshmanan, V. (1997). Detecting rare signatures. In C. H. Dagli (Ed.), *Artificial neural networks in engineering, ANNIE* (pp. 521–526). ASME Press.

Lensburg, T. (1999). Investment behavior under Knightian uncertainty—An evolutionary approach. *Journal of Economic Dynamics and Control, 23*, 1587–1604.

Li, E. (1994). Artificial neural networks and their business applications. *Information Management*.

Lin, T., Horne, B. G., Tino, P., & Giles, C. L. (1996). Learning long-term dependencies in NARX recurrent neural networks. *IEEE Transactions on Neural Networks, 7*(6), 1329–1338.

Looney, C. G. (1996). Advances in feedforward neural networks: Demystifying knowledge acquiring black boxes. *IEEE Transactions on Knowledge and Data Engineering, 8*(2), 211–226.

Maasoumi, E., Khotanzed, A., & Abaye, A. (1994). Artificial neural networks for some macroeconomic series: A first report. *Econometric Reviews, 13*(1), 105–122.

Masters, T. (1994). *Practical neural network recipes in C++*. Academic Press.

McCulloch, W. S., & Pitts, W. (1943). A logical calculus of the ideas immanent in nervous activity. *The Bulletin of Mathematical Biophysics, 5*(4), 115–133.

McMillan, D. (2005). Non-linear dynamics in international stock market returns. *Review of Financial Economics, 14*(1), 81–91.

Meade, N., & Smith, I. (1985). ARARMA vs ARIMA—A study of the benefits of a new approach to forecasting. *Omega, 13*, 519–534.

Me'lard, G., & Pasteels, J. (2000). Automatic ARIMA modeling including interventions, using time series expert software. *International Journal of Forecasting, 16*, 497–508.

Minsky, M., & Pappert, S. (1969). *Perceptrons*. MIT Press.

Minton, S., Carbonell, J. G., Knoblock, C. A., Kuokka, D. R., Etzioni, O., & Gil, Y. (1989). Explanation-based learning: A problem solving perspective. *Artificial Intelligence, 40*(1–3), 63–118.

Moody, J., & Yarvin, N. (1992). Networks with learned unit response functions. In J. Moody (Ed.), *Advances in neural information processing systems* (pp. 1048–1055). Morgan Kaufman.

Ngiam, J., Coates, A., Lahiri, A., Prochnow, B., Le, Q., & Ng, A. (2011). On optimisation methods for deep learning. *Proceedings of the 28th International Conference on Machine Learning* (pp. 265–272). ICML-11.

Nelson, M., & Illingworth, W. (1990). *A practical guide to neural nets*. Addison-Wesley.

Newbold, P., Agiakloglou, C., & Miller, J. (1994). Adventues with ARIMA software. *International Journal of Forecasting, 10*, 573–581.

Newbold, P., & Bos, T. (1989). On exponential smoothing and the assumption of deterministic trend plus white noise data generating models. *International Journal of Forecasting, 5*, 523–527.

Parzen, E. (1982). ARARMA models for time series analysis and forecasting. *Journal of Forecasting, 1*, 67–87.

Pegels, C. (1969). Exponential smoothing: Some new variations. *Management Science, 15*(5), 311–315.

Penrose, R. (1998). Quantum computation, entanglement and state reduction. *Philosophical Transactions of the Royal Society of London. Series A: Mathematical, Physical and Engineering Sciences, 356*(1743), 1927–1939.

Pesaran, M. H., & Timmermann, A. (1995). Predictability of stock returns: Robustness and economic significance. *The Journal of Finance, 50*(4), 1201 1228.

Peterson, G. E., Clair, D. S., Aylward, S. R., & Bond, W. E. (1995). Using Taguchi's method of experimental design to control errors in layered perceptrons. *IEEE transactions on neural networks, 6*(4), 949–961.

Pham, D. (1994). Neural networks in engineering. In G. Rzevski (Ed.), *Applications of artificial intelligence in engineering, AIENG/94, proceedings of the 9th international conference* (pp. 3–36). Computational Mathematics Publications.

Plant, R. E., & Stone, N. D. (1991). *Knowledge-based systems in agriculture*. McGraw-Hill.

Poskitt, D., & Tremayne, A. (1986). The selection and use of linear and bilinear time series models. *International Journal of Forecasting, 2*, 101–114.

Qi, M. (2001). Predicting US recessions with leading indicators via neural networks. *International Journal of Forecasting, 17*, 383–401.

Riesbeck, C. K., & Schank, R. C. (1989). *Inside case-based reasoning*. Lawrence Edbaum Associates.

Rosenblatt, F. (1958). The perceptron: a probabilistic model for information storage and organization in the brain. *Psychological Review, 65*(6), 386.

Rumelhart, D. E., Hinton, G. E., & Williams, R. J. (1985). *Learning internal representations by error propagation*. California Univ. San Diego La Jolla Inst. for Cognitive Science. MIT Press

Sabbatini, M., & Linton, O. (1998). A GARCH model of the implied volatility of the Swiss market index from option prices. *International Journal of Forecasting, 14*, 199–213.

Schalkoff, R. (1997). *Artificial neural networks*. McGraw-Hill.

Shachmurove, Y., & Witkowska, D. (2001). Dynamic interrelation among major work stock market: A neural network analysis. *International Journal of Business Management, 6*(1), 1–22.

Schwartz, T. (1995). Mr. Spock has arrived. *Futures: The magazine of Commodities and Options, 24*(1), 46–48.

Snyder, R. D. (1985). Recursive estimation of dynamic linear statistical models. *Journal of the Royal Statistical Society (B), 47*, 272–276.

South Africa Fintech Vision. (2020). *Intergovernmental Fintech working group*. doi: https://www.moonstone.co.za/upmedia/uploads/library/Moonstone%20Library/MS%20Industry%20News/South_Africa_FinTech_Vision.pdf

Souza, L., & Smith, J. (2002). Bias in the memory for different sampling rates. *International Journal of Forecasting, 18*, 299–313.

Sullivan, R., Timmermann, A., & White, H. (1999). Data-snooping, technical trading rule performance, and the bootstrap. *The journal of Finance, 54*(5), 1647–1691.

Swales, G., & Yoon, Y. (1992). Applying artificial neural networks to investment analysis. *Financial Analysts Journal, 48*, 78–80.

Swanson, N. R., & White, H. (1997). A model selection approach to real-time macroeconomic forecasting using linear models and artificial neural networks. *Review of Economics and Statistics, 79*(4), 540–550.

Swingler, K. (1996). *Applying neural networks: A practical guide*. Morgan Kaufmann.

Tkacz, G. (2001). Neural network forecasting of Canadian GDP growth. *International Journal of Forecasting, 17*, 57–69.

Tong, H. (1983). *Threshold models in non-linear time series analysis* (Vol. 1). Springer Science & Business Media.

Van Gysen, M., Huang, C. S., & Kruger, R. (2013). The performance of linear versus nonlinear models in forecasting returns on the Johannesburg *Stock Exchange*. *International Business & Economics Research Journal (IBER), 12*(8), 985–994.

Vellido, A., Lisboa, P. J., & Vaughan, J. (1999). Neural networks in business: A survey of applications (1992–1998). *Expert Systems with applications, 17*(1), 51–70.

Volterra, V. (1930). *Theory of functionals and of integro-differential equations*. Dover.

von Neumann, J. (1958). *The computer and the brain*. MIT Press.

Weiss, S., & Kulikowski, C. (1991). *Computer systems that learn.* Morgan Kauffman.

Werbos, P. (1974). *Beyond regression: New tools for prediction and analysis in the behavior science.* Unpublished Doctoral Dissertation, Harvard University.

Widrow, B., & Hoff, M. E. (1960). *Adaptive switching circuits.* Stanford University, CA, Stanford Electronics Labs.

Wilson, S. W. (1994). ZCS: A zeroth level classifier system. *Evolutionary Computation, 2*(1), 1–18.

Wythoff, B. (1993). Backpropagation neural networks: A tutorial. *Chemometrics and Intelligent Laboratory Systems, 18*(2), 115–155.

Yule, G. (1927). On the method of investigating periodicities in disturb ed series, with special reference to Wolfer's sunspot numbers. *Philosophical Transactions of the Royal Society London, Series A, 226,* 267–298.

Zupan, J., & Gasteiger, J. (1991). Neural networks: A new method for solving chemical problems or just a passing phase? *Analytica Chimica Acta, 248*(1), 1–30.

Printed in the United States
by Baker & Taylor Publisher Services